52 Weeks of

Ordinary People -

Extraordinary God

by Jody Neufeld

Energion Publications
P. O. Box 841
Gonzalez, FL 32560
850-968-1001
http://energionpubs.com
pubs@energion.com

Ordinary People - Extraordinary God, 52 Weeks of,
by Jody Neufeld
Published by **Energion Publications**.
P.O. Box 841
Gonzalez, FL 32560
Website: http://www.energionpubs.com

Cover Design by PhotoMD (www.photomd.net)
Cover Photograph © Carol Everhart Roper

ISBN: 1-893729-24-9

Dedication

This book and all the ones to come is humbly dedicated
to my Heavenly Father.

Jesus prayed, *"Father, the time has come for you*
to bring glory to your Son,
in order that he may bring glory to you…
I have brought glory to you here on earth
by doing everything you gave me to do. *John 17:1, 4 (CEV)*

Acknowledgements

I thank God for the pastors (shepherds) that God has brought into my life: Rev. Perry Dalton, Dr. Robert McKibben, and Rev. Bruce Sheffield, who, like Jesus, opened their cloaks and showed me their heart for Christ each Sunday morning.

All the "ordinary" people that my Extraordinary God has used to touch my life, molding me like clay on the potter's wheel. I am thankful that God is willing to break me and start again.

My children who have taught me so much about being a child of God: Janet, who truly has the *gift* of faith, John, a gentle warrior for the weak, and James, who showed more Godly courage and peace in his life than most of us know is available to us.

My husband, Henry, who encourages me, teaches me, and loves me because God said so.

Weekly Prayer/Study Groups

As iron sharpens iron, so one man sharpens another.
                                                    Proverbs 27:17
All a man's ways seem right to him, but the LORD weighs the heart.   *Proverbs 21:2*

Weekly study or prayer groups are a VITAL part of discipleship. In these two verses from the book of Proverbs alone I hear the Lord telling me how important it is that I am <u>accountable</u> to other Christians who are also desiring to grow in the Lord. In a small group of fellow believers I will see how God intended His Church to grow as a Body, each member being gifted for the role that He has for them, networking together to support and encourage each other so they can <u>go out</u> into the world to spread the Good News.

This book is designed to give a short devotion that may be used to 'jump start' the group's time together. The content page gives a listing of the 52 weeks with a note of how that particular devotion could be date-sensitive to the time of year. The space to the left of the list allows you to 'check off' a week, giving your group the option to skip around through the book or working your way from front to back.

Like its older sibling, *Daily Devotions of Ordinary People – Extraordinary God*, I have included some short notes on some of the ordinary people who have impacted <u>my</u> life and I encourage your group to take time at each meeting to PRAISE GOD and THANK HIM for the people He has brought into <u>your</u> lives, remembering that it is GOD who is extraordinarily working through these ordinary people.

If your group wants more information on praying the Scriptures, intercessory prayer, and how to continue to grow into a powerful prayer group, *When 3 to 8 Gather* and *I want to Pray!* is part of this series of books published by Energion Publications.

God bless you as you continue to grow by the power of His Holy Spirit and the example of our Lord and Savior, Jesus Christ.
                                                    – Jody Neufeld

52 Weeks of Ordinary People – Extraordinary God

January
_____ Week 1   New Year
_____ Week 2   The impossible IS possible with God.
_____ Week 3   Take ALL my life
_____ Week 4   Thanks and praise

February
_____ Week 5   Soldiers
_____ Week 6   Valentine's Day
An 'ordinary' person: Henry Neufeld
_____ Week 7   Conquering fear
_____ Week 8   James' testimony

March
_____ Week 9   What God says is the truest words about me.
_____ Week 10   Friendship
_____ Week 11   Father's love
_____ Week 12   Praising BEFORE the battle
_____ Week 13   Easter time

April
_____ Week 14   The 'Judas' in my life
_____ Week 15   Taxes!
_____ Week 16   Praying and Forgiveness
_____ Week 17   God heals AND restores
An 'ordinary' person: Janet Butler

May
_____ Week 18   Blessings
_____ Week 19   Children
_____ Week 20   No room to maneuver
_____ Week 21   Evangelism 101
_____ Week 22   Burdens

June
_____ Week 23   Timing is everything!
_____ Week 24   Parenting
An 'ordinary' person: Rev. Perry Dalton
_____ Week 25   Church of the open door
_____ Week 26   Finding a fellowship to call 'home'

July
____ Week 27 4th of July
____ Week 28 Our nation and leaders
____ Week 29 Prayer
____ Week 30 Sharing

August
____ Week 31 Boasting of weaknesses
____ Week 32 a series: 1 of 4
____ Week 33 2 of 4
____ Week 34 3 of 4
____ Week 35 4 of 4

September
____ Week 36 Whose opinion means the most to me?
An 'ordinary' person: Laney Beard
____ Week 37 Repentance
____ Week 38 Grace
____ Week 39 Tests

October
____ Week 40 Prayer chains
____ Week 41 God, do you hear me?
____ Week 42 Rest and restoration
An 'ordinary' person: My mom, Marybelle Grossheider
____ Week 43 Faith and healing
____ Week 44

November
____ Week 45 Election, our nation
____ Week 46 Priorities
____ Week 47 God's timely words
____ Week 48 Amazing things

December
____ Week 49 John Wesley's quadrilateral
____ Week 50 Faith … just faith
____ Week 51 Christmas
____ Week 52 End of the year

Week 1

A new year with possibilities and opportunities has now begun. It seems like just a week ago that I was looking at the year through the same day!

Each and every day, I have a choice: Choose God or choose the world's way of living my life. I sat on the fence for a long time, most of my life actually. I thought I could love God and do pretty much what I wanted the other six days of the week.

Then came that night in July when I knew that Jesus did it all for me, for my sins! All of a sudden the whole 'salvation' concept wasn't just a theory. It was personal. It was about a relationship. If I was to have a relationship with Jesus, then it was going to be more than a once a week conversation! A marriage wouldn't work if the husband and wife only spoke one day a week! Neither, would my relationship with Jesus grow and become the relationship that would finally fill that emptiness that I had always had.

"I am the vine; you are the branches. If a man remains in me and I in him, he will bear much fruit; apart from me you can do nothing. If anyone does not remain in me, he is like a branch that is thrown away and withers; such branches are picked up, thrown into the fire and burned. If you remain in me and my words remain in you, ask whatever you wish, and it will be given you. This is to my Father's glory, that you bear much fruit, showing yourselves to be my disciples. As the Father has loved me, so have I loved you. Now remain in my love."   *John 15:5-9*

Rejoice in the Lord always. I will say it again: Rejoice! Let your gentleness be evident to all. The Lord is near. Do not be anxious about anything, but in everything, by prayer and petition, with thanksgiving, present your requests to God. And the peace of God, which transcends all understanding, will guard your hearts and your minds in Christ Jesus.   *Philippians 4:4-7*

I will start today with God and put my feet in HIS footsteps. There will be no worldly New Year's resolutions. I am just going to open my heart to Jesus and watch what happens!

Questions:
What 'resolutions' have I made in the past? Were they a 'success'?
Is my daily time with God where <u>HE</u> wants it to be? What changes would He like me to make?

When the man heard this, he was sad, because he was very rich.
Jesus saw how sad the man was. SO he said, "It's terribly hard for rich people to get into God's kingdom! In fact, it's easier for a camel to go through the eye of a needle than for a rich person to get into God's kingdom."
When the crowd heard this, they asked, "How can anyone ever be saved?"
Jesus replied, "There are some things that people cannot do, but God can do anything."
Luke 18:23-27(CEV)

There was a very popular worship song a few years ago "All Things Are Possible" (Darlene Zschech. 1997). It was based on this 27th verse from Luke. I sang this song sometimes with tears of hope born of desperation in the circumstances I was in. God heard my voice and I could feel His very presence as He would pick me up off the floor and assure me that He was already walking before me and had all those 'pesky little problems', that seem so HUGE to me, well under control!

And then, as I saw God work in my life and in the lives of those I loved, I would sing the song with joyful abandon! I would put it in my CD player and just dance around the house! I confess to you that someone also gave me a 'bootlegged' copy of the videotape and I so loved watching adults and children alike sing this song. I could see by the expressions on their face that they KNEW that ALL things were possible with God!!

I know what it is to be poor or to have plenty, and I have lived under all kinds of conditions. I know what it means to be full or to be hungry, to have too much or too little. Christ gives me the strength to face anything.
Philippians 4:12-13 (CEV)

Another translation says: *I know how to live on almost nothing or with everything. I have learned the secret of contentment in every situation, whether it be a full stomach or hunger, plenty or want; for I can do everything God asks me to with the help of Christ who gives me the strength and power.* *(TLB)*

Paul wasn't speaking of just physical hunger. Sometimes I hunger for … unconditional love … wisdom and clear sight in a particular circumstance … 'gifting' to accomplish a task I have been given. God is already there. He already knows the need. He can fulfill the need.

You are kind, LORD, so good and merciful.
You protect ordinary people, and when I was helpless,
you saved me and treated me so kindly that I don't need to worry anymore.
Psalm 116:5-7 (CEV)

Questions: What 'impossibles' do I lay at God's feet today? (Write them down and leave space for God's answer.) Join together in agreement for God to do what He knows to do in each situation.
What are some 'impossibles' that BECAME possible because of God?

The things that happened to those people are examples. They were written down to teach us, because we live in a time when all these things of the past have reached their goal. If you think you are strong, you should be careful not to fall. The only temptation that has come to you is that which everyone has. But you can trust God, who will not permit you to be tempted more than you can stand. But when you are tempted, he will also give you a way to escape so that you will be able to stand it...

"We are allowed to do all things," but all things are not good for us to do. "We are allowed to do all things," but not all things help others grow stronger. Do not look out only for yourselves. Look out for the good of others also.

1 Corinthians 10:11-13, 23-24 (NCV)

Are there things in my life that are "permissible" but not beneficial or constructive to my life? I could qualify that and say my 'spiritual' life but my spiritual life <u>IS</u> my life. Maybe it makes me feel better to try to separate my 'spiritual' life from the rest of my life but there really isn't any separation possible. If I want God to be in my life (guide, director, protector) then do I separate my life into rooms and invite Him into some but then turn and say, "Hey, Lord, uh...I gotta go do something in here so why don't You just hang out over there?!"

So as I look at the TOTAL rooms in my life are there 'hairballs' under the bed and 'cobwebs' in the upper corners that while not causing an overt health problem, they are not inviting the Lord into a <u>clean</u> house. <u>AND</u> when I invite others in (to hang around me) whether they are believers or not, they notice the 'dirt' and wonder just what kind of spiritual housekeeper I am!

I don't want my life to be just a place for 'SHOW'. I want my life to be a place that the Lord desires to use it as His dwelling. God is holy. There is no compromise. He comes closer to me as I leave behind the 'sin that so easily entangles' (Hebrews 12:1) and move closer to His holiness. God does not <u>force</u> His glory or His presence on me. He allows me to refuse His invitation. He desires that I choose Him and choose to be holy. He gives me the Holy Sprit that is the 'voice' inside of me reminding me of the Father's words and wisdom. I have all I need to build a temple where God lives. It is a 'glass' temple that allows God to shine forth so that all others see, all that they remember, is Him.

So prepare your minds for service and have self-control. All your hope should be for the gift of grace that will be yours when Jesus Christ is shown to you. Now that you are obedient children of God do not live as you did in the past. You did not understand, so you did the evil things you wanted. But be holy in all you do, just as God the One who called you, is holy. It is written in the Scriptures: "You must be holy, because I am holy."   1 Peter 1:13-16 (NCV)

Questions: <u>Are</u> there things in my life that are "permissible" but not beneficial or constructive to my life?
Are there parts of my life that I do not allow Jesus to have total access?

v.2 O LORD my God, I called to you for help and you healed me.
v. 3 O LORD, you brought me up from the grave; you spared me from going down into the pit.
v.4 Sing to the LORD, you saints of his; praise his holy name.
v.5 For his anger lasts only a moment but his favor lasts a lifetime;
weeping may remain for a night, but rejoicing comes in the morning.

Psalm 30:2-5

Verse 2 of this Psalm is such a statement of fact: "I called and you answered." Period. God <u>did</u> respond. He met my expectation that He would answer.

Verse 3 seems to say that God did even more than I expected. That His grace and mercy kept me from death (physical, emotional, spiritual) and from the "pit" that I was walking toward. I have been in situations that I KNEW was bad news and I seemed to spin in a circle or wander around and not be able to find my footing. The worse case scenario was rushing toward me and I couldn't seem to change course. God saved me.

Verse 4 is a moment of relief and praise. HALLELUJAH!!! God is WORTHY of my praise!

Verse 5 is like a "philosophical review" of the event. I am a sinner. I chose an un-Godly path but I KNOW I am a Child of God, saved by grace. I know that He is a righteous parent – angry when I am disobedient but continues to show me love – may I always know that I am loved. I cry during the discipline. It isn't fun. It isn't fun when I have to go through the consequences of an "unwise" (I'm being kind to myself!) decision. And so I weep.

Joy DOES come. It may not be literally "in the morning" – like 8 or 12 hours from now. When I turn control over to God, joy does come. The "weeping" may last for a 'season' – and that 'season' may be hours, days, weeks, and yes, even years, but JOY, <u>real</u> JOY that has NOTHING to do with my circumstances <u>WILL</u> come. Yes, I argue with God's timing when I am going through the un-joyful time. But I stand and testify today that God's timing <u>IS</u> perfect and the joy, the relief, the "aahhh" of the cool water after being on God's anvil, does come!

Sing a new song to the Lord! Sing it everywhere around the world! Sing out his praises! Bless his name. Each day tell someone that he saves.
Publish his glorious acts throughout the earth. Tell everyone about the amazing things he does. For the Lord is great beyond description, and greatly to be praised. Worship only him among the gods! For the gods of other nations are merely idols, but our God made the heavens! Honor and majesty surround him; strength and beauty are in his Temple.   *Psalm 96:1-6 (TLB)*

I will praise You today, Lord, for: _____
_____
_____
_____

When the foundations are being destroyed, what can the righteous do?"
The LORD is in his holy temple; the LORD is on his heavenly throne.
He observes the sons of men; his eyes examine them.   *Psalm 11:3-4*

What is there to say in the midst of war? What do I say to my friends who have been notified that their son or daughter has been killed in combat? Where will my eyes be when the next terrorist attack comes? Glued to the television or focused on the One who has the power to do something about EVERY situation?

We have seen pictures and reel after reel of what war looks like. We have to hunt for the pictures of soldiers praying, soldiers being baptized in the desert and reporting miraculous events of protection and care. God isn't sleeping through this war. He isn't *distracted* by some other single incident and missing our concerns.

During the days, months, and years ahead, we as Christians have an opportunity to hold up God's banners of truth, hope, compassion, power, and unconditional love. Whether it is family, friends, fellow members of our local church, co-workers, or even unknown people on the street, we are Christ's ambassadors with opportunities to share God's peace that DOES pass understanding through prayer, fellowship, and witnessing to the character of God.

God's temple, His dwelling on earth is ME. It's YOU. We are His temple. We carry His light into the WHOLE world. Jesus said to *"GO into ALL the world"*. Do I think that Jesus spoke carelessly and didn't really mean "ALL"? I must lift my head out of my own little universe and see the opportunities that the Lord has placed in my path. I can do NOTHING without Him. Sharing that testimony in these uncertain days is being a conduit of God's light – His lighthouse – in a world that would want me to believe that all is lost! Just before He died, Jesus said to His disciples and to me,

"I have much more to say to you, more than you can now bear. But when he, the Spirit of truth, comes, he will guide you into all truth. He will not speak on his own; he will speak only what he hears, and he will tell you what is yet to come. He will bring glory to me by taking from what is mine and making it known to you. All that belongs to the Father is mine. That is why I said the Spirit will take from what is mine and make it known to you... "I have told you these things, so that in me you may have peace. In this world you will have trouble. But take heart! I have overcome the world."   *John 16:12-15, 32*

As we pray each day, let us remember to always pray through to the victory that has already been won!

Questions: What prayer concerns can we lift up before God about our nation?
Who do we know 'in harm's way'?

In case someone out there has forgotten, Valentine's Day is just two short days away. Sometimes I think that there is more media pressure to get a gift for this occasion 'RIGHT' than there is at Christmas! Whether you are a guy or a girl, God has a suggestion for the PERFECT GIFT! It is not a dozen roses. It is not a diamond ring, necklace, or bracelet. It is more precious than that. It is FIVE MINUTES of your time in prayer <u>EVERY DAY</u> for your wife or husband or friend. Let's see what Jesus says:

"Have faith in God! If you have faith in God and don't doubt, you can tell this mountain to get up and jump into the sea, and it will. Everything you ask for in prayer will be yours, if you only have faith. Whenever you stand up to pray, you must forgive what others have done to you. Then your Father I heaven will forgive your sins."   *Mark 11:22-25 (CEV)*

Jesus tells us clearly about the <u>power</u> of prayer AND He tells us that the prayer must be coupled with forgiveness. Whether you are married or seeking God's will in a relationship, it is hard work. It <u>requires</u> GOD'S grace and mercy and LOVE each and every day. Prayer is the secret ingredient.

A wonderful Christian author, Stormie Omartian, has written a series of books "The Power of the Praying Wife", "The Power of the Praying Husband", and "The Power of the Praying Parent". I am not working on commission here! But Mrs. Omartian has done a wonderful job in writing down some guidelines for us to help us pray for our spouse and children – regardless if we are <u>going</u> to be married, if we have <u>been</u> married for 1 year or 50, whether our children are infants or 40 years old.

Let us give our loved ones the BEST Valentine ever – lifting them in prayer EVERY DAY. They will know it! They will see and feel the blessings of the Lord in their life as you lift them in prayer. 1 Corinthians 13 from the CEV:

What if I could speak all languages of humans and of angels? If I did not love others, I would be nothing more than a noisy gong or a clanging cymbal. What if I could prophesy and understand all secrets and all knowledge? What if I had faith that moved mountains? I would be nothing, unless I loved others. What if I gave away all that I owned and let myself be burned alive? I would gain nothing, unless I loved others.

Love is kind and patient, never jealous, boastful, proud, or rude. Love isn't selfish or quick tempered. It doesn't keep a record of wrongs that others do. Love rejoices in the truth, but not in evil. Love is always supportive, loyal, hopeful, and trusting. Love never fails.

Everyone who prophesies will stop, and unknown languages will no longer be spoken. All that we know will be forgotten. We don't know everything, and our prophecies are not complete. But what is perfect will someday appear, and what isn't perfect will then disappear.

When we were children, we thought and reasoned as children do. But when we grew up, we quit our childish ways. Now all we can see of God is like a cloudy picture in a mirror. Later we will see him face to face. We don't know everything, but then we will, Justas God completely understands us. For now there are faith, hope, and love. But of these three, the greatest is love.

(continued from Week 6)

Questions: What says 'I love you' most clearly to you?

An Ordinary Person

Henry Neufeld – born in British Columbia, Canada, to missionary parents with a brother and two sisters, Henry spent his early years learning about servant hood and 'being content in all things.' His thirst for knowledge had him continuing his graduate studies in Biblical Languages and coming out of that <u>not</u> believing in God. He took a ten-year tour through the military doing Special Operations and earning the nickname of 'Little Hitler' for his ability to do personnel reviews and cut people down to size! To meet this gentle man now is to come into contact with the power of God to <u>totally</u> change people and make 'head knowledge' <u>about</u> Him become 'heart knowledge' <u>of</u> Him. Henry loves me even in the un-lovable times. He supports me and God's 'call' on <u>my</u> life. He is truly my covenant marriage partner with the Lord.

Elisha's servant got up early, and when he went out, he saw an army with horses and chariots all around the city. The servant said to Elisha, "Who, my master, what can we do?"
Elisha said, "Don't be afraid. The army that fights for us is larger than the one against us."
Then Elisha prayed, "LORD, open my servant's eyes and let him see."
The LORD opened the eyes of the young man, and he saw that the mountain was full of horses and chariots of fire all around Elisha.
                                          2 Kings 6:15-17 (NCV, emphasis mine)

"Oh my Lord, what shall I do?" I've been there – wore that t-shirt down to a rag – and I am here today to testify to the fear that tried to isolate and destroy me.

Fear and deception are the great weapons of the enemy. If he can convince me that I am overwhelmed and outnumbered, then I will give up. I will pull in and try to find some cave to hide away.

"Open His eyes so he may see." That's the answer. Give me eyes to see YOUR truth, Lord. There is not a situation that God does not have control. God is Creator, Ruler, Savior, King of King, Alpha and Omega, beginning and end.

I testify to you today that He has brought me through abuse, shame, poor choices, divorce, raising three children (through their teen years!), ministry, financial catastrophes, cancer, and the list goes on – GOD brought me through. WHO WAS WITH ME WAS GREATER THAN THOSE WHO WERE WITH 'THE OTHER GUY'!!!

The angel of the LORD camps around those who fear God, and he saves them.
Examine and see how good the LORD is. Happy is the person who trusts him. You who belong to the LORD, fear him! Those who fear him will have everything they need.   *Psalm 34:7-9*
When situations seem overwhelming – God hasn't deserted me! In fact, He's gone before me!

Those who go to God Most High for safety will be protected by the Almighty.
I will say to the LORD, "You are my place of safety and protection. You are my God and I trust you.
God will save you from hidden traps and from deadly diseases.
He will cover you with his feathers, and under his wings you can hide. His trust will be your shield and protection.   *Psalm 91:1-4 (NCV)*

God is faithful. Even the darkness of my troubles is like light to Him (Psalm 139). He is ready to meet with me any time of the day or night. When turmoil comes, stopping right then and laying it all out to God will bring peace and clarity to my overloaded mind and spirit. Allowing God to separate truth from lies and shift the priorities to His will produces the strength that I need for the day.

Questions: With thought and <u>total</u> honesty, what are my fears?
Share some times when God was working in a situation even before we knew there was a need.

Give thanks to the LORD and pray to him. Tell the nations what he has done. Sing to him; sing praises to him. Tell about all his miracles. Be glad that you are his; let those who seek the LORD be happy.   *1 Chronicles 16:8-10 (NCV)*

Isn't that a great hymn of praise to God, who is so worthy of praise?! David spoke these words as the Ark of Covenant was brought into Jerusalem. Truly a time of celebration!

But we thank God! He gives us the victory through our Lord Jesus Christ. So my dear brothers and sisters, stand strong. Do not let anything change you. Always give yourselves fully to the work of the Lord, because you know that your work in the Lord is never wasted.   *1 Corinthians 15:57-58 (NCV)*

I am very blessed in my life. I have found our Father God to be faithful. May I briefly testify?

In April 1999, my then 12-year-old son was playing baseball and basketball and had discovered girls weren't as bad as he previously thought. One day, he came to me complaining of a sore throat. I looked. There was…a growth …a tumor. Three weeks later, he was diagnosed with cancer.

Always be joyful. Pray continually, and give thanks whatever happens. That is what God wants for you in Christ Jesus.   *1 Thessalonians 5:16-18 (NCV)*

For the next year, that kind of Scripture was hard for me to read, much less claim and agree. For the next year, my son and I went every week for chemo and every three weeks it would require chemo in the hospital. Four weeks of radiation treatment would cause 2nd degree burns on in the inside of his mouth. No school. No baseball or basketball. No hair. Weight loss. Some visits with friends when he wasn't too sick or too weak or having treatments or transfusions or…whatever. God is faithful and He is worthy of my praise.

Hundreds, no <u>thousands</u> of people prayed. I received emails from all over the world, as one person would tell another. We had compassionate doctors, nurses, technicians, and volunteers, who treated us like we were the only one they would care for that day. We had a family of God that held our arms up (like Aaron and Hur did for Moses) when we were too tired to pray for ourselves. God is faith and He is worthy of my praise.

I know how to live when I am poor, and I know how to live when I have plenty. I have learned the secret of being happy at any time in everything that happens, when I have enough to eat and when I go hungry, when I have more than I need and when I do not have enough. I can do all things through Christ, because he give me strength.   *Philippians 4:12-13 (NCV)*

I will not lie to you and tell you that I live these Scriptures. I continue to press in closer to Jesus to learn from Him and His friends.

My son was healed, miraculously and by God. The enemy, satan, would try to remind us of all that we do not have; of our troubles, all our unanswered questions…especially the 'whys'. But what about all the many, many blessings He gives us? He has given me trust…that step beyond faith…where I believe in Him no matter what I 'see' or what the situation. He gives peace beyond understanding. God is faithful and He is worthy of my praise.

Suggestion: Share Scripture that is 'hard' for you right now.

Week 9

I am pleading for your help, O Lord; for I have been honest and have done what is right, and you must listen to my earnest cry! Publicly acquit me, Lord, for you are always fair. You have tested me and seen that I am good. You have come even in the night and found nothing amiss and know that I have told the truth...

Protect me as you would the pupil of your eye; hide me in the shadow of your wings as you hover over me. My enemies encircle me with murder in their eyes..

Lord, arise and stand against them. Push them back! Come and save me from these men of the world whose only concern is earthly gain – these men whom you have filled with your treasures so that their children and grandchildren are rich and prosperous.

But as for me, my contentment is not in wealth but in seeing you and knowing all is well between us. And when I awake in heaven, I will be fully satisfied, for I will see you fact to face.   *Psalm 17:1-3, 8-9, 13-15 (TLB)*

Have you ever wanted vindication? I can raise my hand on that! Whether it's "winning" a discussion with my husband or seeing MY baseball team annihilate a rival, I have desired <u>vindication</u>.

<u>Validation</u> is a close cousin to <u>vindication</u>. Many times they travel together. When I am vindicated, my worth, my integrity, I might even say, my name, is validated.

David, or this psalm writer, humbly cries out to God because He knows THAT is where His vindication will come! Linda Smith, a woman of God who has mentored youth for many years, tells the young people, "What God says about you is the most true thing about you".

Who I am, what I am worth is not defined by my job, my boss, my family, parents, the people I call friends, or even the church that I attend. So anything that they might say against me – what do I care? If God didn't say it – it isn't totally true!

What God says about me – now those are defining words:

For I am God – I only – and there is no other like me who can tell you what is going to happen. All I say will come to pass, for I do whatever I wish. I will call that swift bird of prey from the east – that man Cyrus from far away. And he will come and do my bidding. I have said I would do it and I will.

Isaiah 46:10-11 (TLB)

Dear friends, let us practice loving each other, for love comes from God and those who are loving and kind show that they are getting to know him better. But if a person isn't loving and kind, it shows that he doesn't know God – for God is love.

God showed how much he loved us by sending his only Son into this wicked world to bring to us eternal life through his death. In this act we see what real love is: it is not our love for God, but his love for us when he sent his Son to satisfy God's anger against our sins.   *1 John 4:7-12 (TLB)*

Questions: Who does God say I am?
What does He say about me in Scripture?

What <u>is</u> a friend? A friendship is truly an 'open' relationship. Unlike marriage, there is no legal binding or separating of the relationship. But like marriage, it will last a long time and produce wondrous fruit if I allow God to make the choices, set the standards, and be the binding that causes it to grow for many years. Let's see what God says about friends. Proverbs is a good place to start.

Gossip is no good! It causes hard feelings and comes between friends.
Proverbs 16:28 (CEV)

Sounds like I need to be careful whom I listen to! Does the one that I call 'friend' speak constructively of other people or does he/she constantly find fault with everyone? If she is a faultfinder – it will sure makes me wonder what she may say about <u>me</u> when I'm not around! Also, is there a spirit of loyalty to the friends that God has given me? I need to remember that what <u>God</u> says about me or about my friends is the truest thing – not the 'gossip' that is spoken by others!

A friend is always a friend, and relatives are born to share our troubles.
Proverbs 17:17 (CEV)

In good times and tough times, the friend that God has brought into my life loves me in spite of myself. That person sees me as a 'work in progress' and rejoices when I repent and grow in faith. They take their cue from God and forgive <u>and</u> forget!

Some friends don't help, but a true friend is closer than your own family.
Proverbs 18:24 (CEV)

This is a 'hard Word' from the Lord. It tells me that God is sending me friends that will walk as Jesus did. I remember when I came to realize that while I would always care about my friends, those that I had known for many years, even from childhood, but that there were some that I was going to have to 'cut loose'. Jesus was not a #1 priority in their life and they led a life that was MY 'old life' and I couldn't sit on the fence anymore. I could care about them and pray for them but I couldn't hang with them anymore. Many of them couldn't accept the 'new Jody'. It was a very painful time. Some have remained in touch and we can 'agree…to disagree' about many things. Others decided that the change was too much and so they have left.

You can trust a friend who corrects you, but kisses from an enemy are nothing but lies. *Proverbs 27:6 (CEV)*

This might be translated that the truth from a friend is always better than flattery from an enemy. An arrow from God, 'shot', so to speak, through a friend can bring about a painful truth but the Holy Spirit will confirm God's truth to me and I will be glad and rejoice in that friend who was obedient to speak what the Lord gave them…speaking always in love.

I'm going to stop right now and pray for my God-given friends. I am going to pray that God will bless them with all that they need to come closer to Him and know Him more intimately.

Questions: What makes a friend more than an acquaintance or neighbor?

You had my mother give birth to me. You made me trust you while I was just a baby. I have leaned on you since the day I was born; you have been my God since my mother gave me birth.   *Psalm 22:9-10 (NCV)*

I have been reading a book, <u>Experiencing the Father's Embrace</u> by Jack Frost. He and his wife minister to pastors and leadership, having a vision that we would all 'see' the total love that our Father has for us. One of the anonymous stories he relates was when a couple came for prayer with two small sons. The woman wept as she confessed that she did not know how to love. She had never experienced the unconditional love of a father and so she had no point of reference to give the same to her children. Her five-year-old son innocently turned to her and told her that <u>he</u> would show her how to love.

I am easily frustrated when I am asked to do something I don't know how to do. I sense this mother was feeling that kind of frustration. Jesus knew I would have days like that and He spoke words just for those times.

At that time the followers came to Jesus and asked, "Who is greatest in the kingdom of heaven?"

Jesus called a little child to him and stood the child before his followers. Then he said, "I tell you the truth, you must change and become like little children. Otherwise, you will never enter the kingdom of heaven. The greatest person in the kingdom of heaven is the one who makes himself humble like this child."

Matthew 18:1-4 (NCV)

When a child doesn't know something, he/she will tug on your sleeve and *ASK* for help! It is a simple equation to them – I don't know so I ask someone who does and then I'll know. Period.

When I do not know how to <u>receive</u> the Father's love, I can take my clue from someone who does, a child, and just hold my arms out and take it in. When a child receives a parent's love, there are no barriers or preconceived ideas about how it will be delivered, he/she just knows it's coming and they hold their arms wide open and just receive it!

When I do not know how to <u>give</u> the Father's love, I can take my clue from someone who does, Jesus, who like a child, throws His arms out without any barriers or preconceived ideas about how it will flow out, and He just lets it happen!

Receiving must come before the giving and it is so, SO important that I take the time to allow my Father to pour out His love on me. I need nutrients for my physical body. I need 'Father love' for my spiritual life.

Let's just stop and be quiet and <u>receive</u> our Heavenly Father's love. Shhh.

Suggestion: Sit for <u>at least</u> five minutes *quietly*, listening.
Read Jeremiah 31:3 and Psalm 139

Week 12

Psalm 22 v. 3 tells me that God inhabits – lives – in the praise of His people. The power of God is present when I praise Him.

Early the next morning, as everyone got ready to leave for the desert near Tekoa, Jehoshaphat stood up and said, "Listen my friends, if we trust the LORD God and believe what these prophets have told us, the LORD will help us, and we will be successful."

Then he explained his plan and appointed men to march in front of the army and praise the LORD for his holy power by singing: "Praise the LORD! His love never ends."

As soon as they began singing, the LORD confused the enemy camp, so that the Ammonite and Moabite troops attacked and completely destroyed those from Edom. Then they turned against each other and fought until the entire camp was wiped out!...

Jehoshaphat led the crowd back to Jerusalem. And as they marched, they played harps and blew trumpets. They were very happy because the LORD had given them victory over their enemies, so when they reached the city, they went straight to the temple.

When the other nations heard how the LORD had fought against Judah's enemies, they were too afraid to invade Judah. The LORD let Jehoshaphat's kingdom be at peace. 2 Chronicles 20:20-23, 27-30 (CEV)

King Jehoshaphat was obedient to a pretty risky order that he got from God. Send singers and musicians and dancers out in front of the army. Praise God before the battle even begins.

How does that work in my life? Well, how do I usually react when tough times come in my life? Do I think about calling my close brothers and sisters to come pray with me or do I think they'd be too busy? Do I check to see when – even how many times – I can go to church and attend worship and enter in to a time with the Lord and body of Believers or do I crawl into my hole at home and pull the covers over my head? Do I turn on my CD player for praise and worship music, seeking to get my 'eternal eyes' back on track, allowing God to guide me out of the pit, or do I turn on the TV to lose myself in whatever sitcom – never to be seen again that day in God's presence. Jesus is waiting to sit down and hear my woes and help me sift through the truth with the power of His Holy Spirit – if I will just choose that option!

Even more importantly, if I will make praising God the first priority of each day, then I AM praising Him before any battle begins. I have a friend of mine named Janet, who gets up each morning and spends an hour or so outside in her backyard just walking and talking with the Lord. But her children and husband tell me that she also has been known to dance and leap across the yard as she praises her heavenly Father who made this glorious day. What a testimony!

Questions: What are some of the ways to start the day with God?
What are some battles where I need 'praise help'?

Week 13

It was almost time for the Feast of Unleavened Bread, called the Passover Feast. The leading priests and teachers of the law were trying to find a way to kill Jesus, because they were afraid of the people.

Satan entered Judas Iscariot, one of Jesus' twelve apostles. Judas went to the leading priests and some of the soldiers who guarded the Temple and talked to them about a way to hand Jesus over to them. They were pleased and agreed to give Judas money. He agreed and watched for the best time to hand Jesus over to them when he was away from the crowd.

The Day of Unleavened Bread came when the Passover lambs had to be sacrificed. Jesus said to Peter and John, "Go and prepare the Passover meal for us to eat."...So Peter and John left and fond everything as Jesus had said. And they prepared the Passover meal.   *Luke 22:1-8, 13 (NCV)*

I remember as a child helping my mom prepare the Easter Sunday dinner. Most of the preparation happened on Friday and Saturday because the meal base was ham, potato salad, and deviled eggs. My usual task was to cube all the cooked potatoes. A messy, sticky job! And I suspect there is some preparation needed for a Passover dinner also. If you do not have your own large room then you have to find someone who is willing to 'rent' you one. Peter and John must have been pretty happy to find things already in place for them. Not only a big enough table but enough comfortable couches for everyone to recline. Nice!

Judas had another job. I like Luke's account of this because he puts the <u>primary</u> blame where it belongs – satan! I wonder what was in Judas' mind. What lies were being whispered as a justification for betraying someone who had treated him with kindness and love? When I am tempted and choose to agree – logic doesn't become part of the equation.

The account of Jesus' last supper with His disciples is about their relationship. Jesus knows that time is short and no matter which gospel I read there are important points for me to take into my heart. Matthew and Mark give me a beautiful picture of the breaking of the bread and sharing of the wine as Jesus testifies that He won't personally do this again with us until He returns. He promises He will return in glory. Jesus also reminds me through Peter that I, too, will deny Him but He died for me anyway! Luke reports the question among the disciples as to who is the greatest and He reminds them that He has been their servant. He also tells Peter that there will be a time of sifting but that He has already prayed for him to be strong. What an encouragement that during <u>my</u> times of 'sifting' that Jesus is there praying for me! John tells of the washing of the disciples' feet and then writes four mores chapters worth of encouragement and concludes with Jesus' prayer in chapter 17.

We might think that Holy Thursday or Maundy Thursday is about the Last Supper, Holy Communion. That is the sacrament. A sacrament is "an outward sign of an inward change". Communion is all about the relationship between Jesus and me. It is about <u>OUR</u> communing together. There is so much there for me to receive – if I will just 'recline' with Him and listen.

Suggestion: Read John 19, sharing your thoughts about what Jesus did for you.

Week 14

Jesus knew on the evening of Passover Day that it would be his last night on earth before returning to his Father. During supper the devil had already suggested to Judas Iscariot, Simon's son, that this was the night to carry out his plan to betray Jesus. Jesus knew that the Father had given him everything and that he had come from God and would return to God. And how he loved his disciples! So he got up from the supper table, took off his robe, wrapped a towel around his loins, poured water into a basin, and began to wash the disciples' feet and to wipe them with the towel he had around him. When he came to Simon Peter, Peter said to him, "Master, you shouldn't be washing our feet like this!" Jesus replied, "You don't understand now why I am doing it; some day you will." "No!" Peter protested, "you shall never wash my feet!" "But if I don't you can't be my partner," Jesus replied. Simon Peter exclaimed, "Then wash my hands and head as well – not just my feet!"...

"You call me 'Master' and 'Lord,' and you do well to say it, for it is true. And since I, the Lord and Teacher, have washed your feet, you ought to wash each other's feet. I have given you an example to follow: do as I have done to you. How true it is that a servant is not greater than his master. Nor is the messenger more important than the one who sends him. You know these things – now do them! That is the path of blessing."　　　　　*John 13:1-9, 13-17 (TLB)*

This is John's account of the passion of Jesus Christ. The apostle, John, was the only one who wrote about Jesus washing his disciples feet. John seems to really want us to grab hold of the immense scope of Jesus' love.

In looking at several versions of this scripture passage, I did not find any clear statement that Judas left the room prior to the foot washing or the breaking of the bread for communion. It is difficult for me to accept that Jesus got down on His hands and knees and washed the feet of the man He KNEW was going to betray Him. And yet, that is why Jesus came. To love the unlovable. To be a servant to those who hated Him, even betrayed Him.

"And so I am giving a new commandment to you now – love each other just as much as I love you. Your strong love for each other will prove to the world that you are my disciples."　　　　　*John 13:34-35 (TLB)*

Who is the Judas in my life? I suspect we all have at <u>least</u> one. It may be an ex-spouse. It may be a child who has stolen from us, betrayed us. It may be a parent who has abused us. It may be a co-worker who 'set us up', made us look bad, took credit for our idea. It may even be a member of our church who has betrayed us, treated us worse than a non-believer! Jesus is asking <u>ME</u> to wash Judas' feet. Wash them tenderly, thoroughly, and anoint them with God's oil of love.

Father, I need Your grace here. I receive Your 'call' to this service. I ask, Father, that You show me Jesus washing <u>MY</u> feet. My dirty, unworthy feet. Father, You know me. You know, that like Peter, I need my head and hands washed, too! Wash me clean, Father, of my pride and self-righteousness, that I may truly be Your servant, glorify <u>YOU</u> in everything that I do. I ask this in Jesus' name. AMEN.

Suggestion: Begin today to pray for someone that may fit this picture.

Week 15

First, I tell you to pray for all people, asking God for what they need and being thankful to him. Pray for rulers and for all who have authority so that we can have quiet and peaceful lives full of worship and respect for God. This is good, and it pleases God our Savior, who wants all people to be saved and to know the truth.   *1 Timothy 2:1-4 (NCV)*

April 15th is probably the day when more complaining and whining occurs than any other day in the United States. Some may have their day earlier in the year if they file their taxes sooner. Others may experience this phenomenon more often if they file taxes quarterly and/or read their accountant's report. Most of us in America enjoy our freedom and prosperity but we hate paying the price! We are quick to find fault with 'the system' or 'the President' or 'Congress'.

Paul and Timothy lived in a time where whining and complaining against the government could get you imprisoned, even killed. It is unfortunate that there are still places where that are true today. Paul suggests prayers of thanksgiving and petitions for change be given to <u>God</u> who is able to bring about the changes that produce that righteousness (right relationship) which in turns brings holiness and godliness to the land.

I don't know the spiritual state of my local or national figures. I cannot make that determination even by what they claim. No matter who they are or what they claim, God says I should pray for them. I should pray for them whether I like their policies or not. I should ask God to bless them with His presence and wisdom and mercy whether I like them or not!

[The Pharisees said,] *"So tell us what you think. Is it right to pay taxes to Caesar or not?" But knowing that these leaders were trying to trick him, Jesus said, "You hypocrites! Why are you trying to trap me? Show me a coin used for paying the tax." So the men showed him a coin. Then Jesus asked, "Whose image and name are on the coin?" The men answered, "Caesars." Then Jesus said to them,"Give to Caesar the things that are Caesar's, and give to God the things that are God's." When they heard what Jesus said, they were amazed and left him and went away.*   *Matthew 22:17-22 (NCV)*

When God blessed me with provision to care for my family, did I think He didn't realize that there was an 'income tax' involved? Is God's hand so short that He is not going to provide for me in <u>every</u> way?

In another passage in Matthew 17, Peter comes to Jesus when the collectors come to him to get the Temple Tax. Peter, I suspect, is hoping that Jesus will give them a good Scripture that will say that because they are doing 'ministry for the Lord' they are not subject to pay. Let's be clear here. The passage is talking about the tax that was required by the <u>temple</u> for its upkeep. That being said, Jesus infers that He doesn't approve of the way the tax is levied but He also does <u>not</u> sanction disobedience. God provides the way to pay it.

I want to pray for the leadership in my city, my county, my state, and my country each day that God will guide and direct them in <u>His</u> ways. Most of all that we continue to have FREEDOM of faith so that <u>all</u> will have the opportunity to know Him and come to the knowledge of His truth.

Question: Who are your local leaders and what prayers can you offer daily?

In the morning, O LORD, you hear my voice;
  in the morning I lay my requests before you
   and wait in expectation.   *Psalm 5:3*

This life, or anyone in it, can NEVER meet all my expectations. When I put my expectations in the Lord and know that my help comes from Him. That surely takes the pressure off those around me! It is God's desire that I rely fully on Him. Relying on solely others will bring only bitterness and un-forgiveness. Relying on God brings hope and peace with the assurance that the Lord will hold and sustain me.

"If you forgive others for the wrongs they do to you, your Father in heaven will forgive you. But if you don't forgive others, your Father will not forgive your sins."   *Matthew 6:14-15 (CEV)*

Forgiveness. Yes, I will definitely say that I need to pray for forgiveness. Oh – Lord! You want me to pray that I will forgive OTHERS?!

During some of the most difficult times of my life, forgiving others was the second hardest thing to do. I think it goes along with the 'expectation thing' that we just talked about. People hurt me. They're human! But when it is people who are closest to me – husband, parents, children – even a pastor or fellow Believer – it seems to add a layer that makes forgiveness just a bit more difficult. I 'expect' more, don't I? Even though He doesn't need it – I admit that sometimes I even need to forgive GOD! Forgiveness removes the root of bitterness that can grow branches of offense and depression, etc. etc. and blocks God's joy from my life.

And then there's the hardest thing I need to pray to receive – God's grace to forgive MYSELF!!! It's the pits when I think that I have failed or I'm responsible for a bad thing that has happened. Maybe I really haven't failed but I let regret and condemnation pound away at me. Someone recently said that as a child of God "I may fail but I am NOT a failure!". This is a weight I was NEVER meant to carry. "Could've and should've and would've" are SOOOO counterproductive!

Prayer IS communication with God. It is my time to lay it all out for God. Yes, He DOES already know what's going on in my life and going through my mind but laying it out – verbalizing it or journaling it – is the beginning of my releasing it. It is also my time to LISTEN to God. Hear Him speak to me. Yes, even audibly but also in His written word, the Scriptures, and in His Holy Spirit to my spirit.

The result is peace, encouragement, forgiveness, thanksgiving, joy comfort, and love. Praying is a good thing!

Questions: Share some ways God has given you mercy (unconditional forgiveness).
Who do you need to forgive?

Week 17

Simon Peter, Thomas, Nathanael, the sons of Zebedee, and two others of his disciples were together. Simon Peter said to them, "I am going fishing." They said to him, "We will go with you." They went out and got into the boat, but that night they caught nothing.

Just as day was breaking, Jesus stood on the shore; yet the disciples did not know that it was Jesus. Jesus said to them, "Children, do you have any fish?" They answered him, "No." He said to them, "Cast the net on the right side of the boat, and you will find some." So they cast it, and now they were not able to haul it in, because of the quantity of fish. The disciple whom Jesus loved therefore said to Peter, "It is the Lord!" When Simon Peter heard that it was the Lord, he put on his outer garment, for he was stripped for work, and threw himself into the sea. The other disciples came in the boat, dragging the net full of fish, for they were not far from the land...   *John 21:2-8 (ESV)*

Peter was grieving. He was grieving, not only for the death of his teacher and friend, but for the dream that JESUS was the Messiah. And so he did what I have done when I grieve...tasks that are familiar and comforting. Fishing had been his way of making a living all of his life. It was also where he first met Jesus. (Matthew 4:18) There was comfort in visiting that place again.

Casting the net, pulling it in, casting it again. There was a rhythm and a good sweat that comes with the work. And just like that time some three years ago, Peter was having no luck fishing. I can see him shaking his head and the sheen of tears that comes to his eyes. "What else? I can't even catch fish!" Peter had just been through the worse days and nights of his life beginning with Jesus' arrest and going straight to the pits when he denied that he knew Jesus not just once but THREE TIMES! I bet he could still see the look that he exchanged with Jesus across Pilate's courtyard. (Luke 22:61) His salty tears mix with the salt spray of the sea.

Once again, Jesus inquires about Peter's luck fishing. Once again, Jesus asks Peter to throw his unsuccessful net back into the sea. "Try it again – this time with me!" is His unstated command. And once again, Peter and his fishing buddies come up with a catch that is SO HUGE it almost sinks the boat!

John's cry, "It is the Lord!" sends Peter over the side of the boat because he cannot wait another minute to get near his Savior, the Savior that once again has saved him and is now going to serve him. Again.

The story doesn't end here. John goes on to tell us that Jesus receives Peter back and the slate is wiped clean. All denials are forgotten. Simon is once again Peter, the rock.

This is the disciple who is bearing witness about these things, and who has written these things, and we know that his testimony is true. Now there are also many other things that Jesus did. Were every one of them to be written, I suppose that the world itself could not contain the books that would be written.

                    John 21:24-25 (ESV)

The world is not big enough to tell the many stories of how Jesus heals and restores. These devotions are not big enough to tell the many times that Jesus has healed me and restored me. JESUS CHRIST BE PRAISED!

(continued from Week 17)

Suggestion: List some of the stories of Jesus healing and restoring.
Take time to pray for yourself and others who need to receive Jesus'
healing, restoring touch today.

An Ordinary Person

Janet Butler – a wife and mother of two beautiful grown daughters, Janet is
passionate about her relationship with Jesus. We met while attending the same
church and watched our children change from rebellious to reverent when God
touched their lives during the 1995 'Pensacola Outpouring'. Those of us who
know her know that Janet is wonderfully gifted by God in the area of prayer.
She has been given a tender, compassionate heart especially toward the children
of God who are hurt and/or lost. Janet would tell you that she certainly is just an
"ordinary" woman used by her "extraordinary" God.

Week 18

Don't be deceived, my beloved brothers and sisters. Every good and complete gift comes down from above, from the Father of lights, with whom there is no variation or even a shadow of turning. James 1:16-17 (HNT)

I've been thinking about blessings lately. Counting my blessings is taking time to have an intimate, personal 'testimony' time with my Lord. I need to do it every day. But do I miss recognizing some of the blessings? My 'world' of sight and sound is a deluge of what advertisers and others think I should have and so my mind easily makes a LONG list of what I don't have. BUT – I AM rich!

God raised us up and made us sit in heavenly places with Christ Jesus, so that he might show in the ages to come the superabundant riches of his grace in kindness to us through Christ Jesus. Ephesians 2:6-7 (HNT)

Yes, I have LIFE in Jesus. That in itself would be enough but there is more. And this is where the victory comes for me. In my day-to-day, moment-to-moment life, I confess that I need to 'see' a tangible blessing that has a 'now' pay off. I know that is shallow of me and shows that my eyes are not always looking with eternal rewards but … there it is! I am blessed:

- ✓ with friends. These friends call me or email me at just the right moment. They pray for me and usually don't tell me.
- ✓ with family. I have a true-blue husband who is not only there in the good days and the victory days but all the days in between. I have children that continue to surprise me with the depth of their lives. I have a brother who even after 50 years still loves his little sister.
- ✓ with a home. I have a car. I am able to go to the grocery store this week.
- ✓ that this morning I didn't spill the sugar. I don't mean a teaspoon. It was almost 2 lbs.!

Blessings come in many sizes and with immediate and long-term consequences. Blessings are gifts from God. They are the manifestation of His grace and mercy. They are gifts just for me. Gifts are nothing when they are left in the bag or kept wrapped up in pretty paper and a bow. Gifts are true gifts when they are opened and appreciated and thanksgiving is given. AND when the gift is seen or used each day. A good reason to think about my blessings every day, isn't it? I bet my conscious list of what I should have or don't have will get smaller and smaller!

So since we have been made right by faith, we have peace with God through our Lord Jesus Christ, through whom we also have received access by faith into this grace by which we stand and boast in the hope of the glory of God. And not in this alone, but we also boast in our tribulations, since we know that tribulation brings out patience, and patience creates character and character produces hope. But hope is not ashamed, because the love of God has been poured out in our hearts through the Holy Spirit which was given to us. Romans 5:1-5 (HNT)

Suggestion: Begin with 'A' and mention a blessing from God for each letter in the alphabet. [crunchy, sweet apples or my grandson, Alex]

Jesus and his followers went to Capernaum. When they went into a house there, he asked them, "What were you arguing about on the road?" But the followers did not answer, because their argument on the road was about which one of them was the greatest. Jesus sat down and called the twelve apostles to him. He said, "Whoever wants to be the most important must be last of all and servant of all."

Then Jesus took a small child and had him stand among them. Taking the child in his arms, he said, "Whoever accepts a child like this in my name accepts me. And whoever accepts me accepts the One who sent me." Mark 9:33-37 (NCV)

Jesus makes it very clear that children are important. In these verses from Mark's gospel, He holds the child in His strong, protective arms as He looks all the adults in the eye and tells them that if they're going to be one of <u>His</u> followers, then pay attention to the needs of this child. And in fact, these children are not only important to Him – but to His Father.

So – where do children rank in our church budget? When we plan special events in our church, how many are geared with special consideration for our children? Does the event give them an opportunity to praise God in <u>their</u> way with <u>their</u> music or must they be quiet and sit through an hour of more of music and text that is relevant to ME?!!

Jesus said to his followers, "Things that cause people to sin will happen, but how terrible for the person who causes them to happen! It would be better for you to be thrown into the sea with a large stone around your neck than to cause one of these little ones to sin. So be careful!

If another follower sins, warn him, and if he is sorry and stops sinning, forgive him. If he sins against you seven times in one day and says he is sorry each time, forgive him." Luke 17:1-4 (NCV)

I hear Jesus remind me that His children are young – in age but also in their relationship to Him. They are looking to ME to be HIS example. I am warned to be careful about the example, about the message I send to these children. Jesus doesn't qualify these children and my responsibility to them only as it applies to my biological children and grandchildren. I am to look with Jesus' eyes to <u>ALL</u> His babies in the faith whether they are 6 or 60!!!

Jesus takes it further, making it clear that while His children NEED discipline, learning obedience and submission to the Father, they also NEED to know the Father's unconditional love and forgiveness. When this younger brother or sister in the Lord SINS and then asks forgiveness, I am to be there with open arms and speak those words of forgiveness, even if that is seven times in one day!

...but Jesus said, "Let the little children come to me. Don't stop them, because the kingdom of heaven belongs to people who are like these children."

Matthew 19:14 (NCV)

Children who need prayer: _____

_____

Week 20

Then Nebuchadnezzar, in a terrible rage, ordered Shadrach, Meshach, and Abednego to be brought in before him. "Is it true, O Shadrach, Meshach, and Abednego," he asked, "that you are refusing to serve my gods or to worship the golden statue I set up? I'll give you one more chance. When the music plays, if you fall down and worship the statue, all will be well. But if you refuse, you will be thrown into a flaming furnace within the hour. And what god can deliver you out of my hands then?"

Shadrach, Meshach, and Abednego replied, "O Nebruchadnezzar, we are not worried about what will happen to us. If we are thrown into the flaming furnace, our God is able to deliver us; and he will deliver us out of your hand, Your Majesty. But if he doesn't, please understand, sir, that even then we will never under any circumstance serve your gods or worship the golden statue you have erected."
Daniel 3:13-18 (TLB)

This is one of those days when I wondered about God!!! I mean, more than usual!!!

This Scripture from Daniel is one of my favorites that I need to read more often. Here were three men who are seemingly without power in their lives, at the mercy of a foreign king. They were ordered to do something that they KNOW they are not going to do. There is no 'wiggle room' here! Refusing to worship the king's god means they were going to die! These three men came back to the king with three short points: 1) They were not worried about defending themselves – they were not pleading for mercy. 2) They said, "Our God Jehovah is able to save us and He WILL do it. And 3) IF it is our God Jehovah's will not to do so, -- we will not serve your god any way"!!!

The story continues with the king REALLY getting angry and heating the furnace so hot that it kills his guards. The three men walk among the flames with a 'mysterious' 4th man and come out of the furnace without even the smell of smoke on their clothes. The king receives an AWESOME testimony and is changed as well as the three men receiving leadership positions in the country.

But all these things that I once thought very worthwhile – now I've thrown them all away so that I can put my trust and hope in Christ alone. Yes, everything else is worthless when compared with the priceless gain of knowing Christ Jesus my Lord.
Philippians 3:7-8 (TLB)

Paul shares his heart. He TOTALLY opens up and reveals that all that he was and is – counts for NOTHING – ZERO – in the presence of his relationship to Christ. Paul knows that his faith in Christ, the salvation that came from that and everything else is from God and THAT is all that matters in his life. He confesses that he has not truly grabbed on to all that the gift of salvation means – but he wants to grab on to it – he wants the prize! That spoke to me today that NOTHING – NOTHING – NOTHING – in my life could compare to the Good News. Zip. Nuttin', honey! As I sit here today and look around at my home, family pictures, the peace of living in the USA, having an income that provides…I consider it a 'throwaway' compared to _knowing_ that Jesus is MY Lord and Savior.

Question: What is it that I must let go of – so I can grab on to Jesus FIRST?

I will always praise the LORD. With all my heart, I will praise the LORD. Let all who are helpless, listen and be glad. Honor the LORD with me! Celebrate his great name. I asked the LORD for help, and he saved me from all my fears...

When his people pray for help, he listens and rescues them from their troubles. The LORD is there to rescue all who are discouraged and have given up hope. The LORD's people may suffer a lot, but he will always bring them safely through.   *Psalm 34:1-4, 17-19 (CEV)*

Late one Sunday night, a man (Kenny) came into the church I was attending. It was during our prayer ministry time. He sat down with his head in his hands. He had been hitchhiking and the smell of alcohol and marijuana was strong on him.

After talking quietly with him for a time, we asked if we could anoint him and pray for him and he agreed. In fact, it seemed like he had experienced this before. As we continued to talk later, he said he had "been a born-again Christian for over 20 years". "I'm not perfect," he said.

Give me your tired, your poor, your huddled masses yearning to be free...

The Statue of Liberty

My own great-great grandparents came to America on a boat tired and poor, yearning to be free from what was then Prussia. Thousands came into the harbors of the United States and found a new life. They came very long distances, making a step of faith that the unknown they were coming towards must be better than the hardships they were leaving.

What about the 'Kenny's' that are coming toward the beacon of Jesus here on earth...His Church? Kenny was tired, poor, and yearning to be free. Do I welcome him into the light of God's presence? That same light that drew me in? Maybe I smelled a little better than Kenny. Maybe my 'sin' wasn't as apparent but I was certainly dirty and smelly in God's eyes.

Kenny had heard about the Way to Jesus. He could quote the Bible verses but was too hurt and afraid or felt too unworthy to accept the free gift into his heart...yearning...but not free...yet.

I believe we are ALL called to be evangelists. When I accepted Jesus as my Savior, I also accepted His command to *"Go...and make disciples"*. WHERE I evangelize is for God to direct. Evangelism could be here in the U.S. or anywhere in the world. OR it could be in my own home church. There are many sitting in the pews of the church that do NOT know Jesus as Savior, their personal Savior. They do not live in freedom that comes with the assurance of their salvation. Some of them are well-dressed and clean and been members for 30 years. Some are a 'Kenny' and come in out of the darkness one night. They have a divine appointment. God have mercy on us if we put out the 'Do not disturb' sign!!!

The LORD then stood beside Samuel and called out as he had done before, "Samuel! Samuel!" "I'm listening," Samuel answered. "What do you want me to do?"   *1 Samuel 3:10 (CEV)*

I am listening to You, Lord. **What do You want me to do?**

"Comfort! Comfort my People!" God says. Speak to Jerusalem's heart, and cry out to her that her warfare is completed, that her iniquity is paid for...
For she has received from the hand of the LORD, double for all her sins.
Do you not know? Have you not heard? The LORD, the eternal God, Creator of the world from end to end, does not grow weary or get tired, there's no searching out his wisdom. He gives strength to the weary, to the one without power he multiples strength. Even young men become tired and grow weary, and youths will surely stumble. But those who put their hope in the LORD renew their strength, they will climb with wings like eagles. They will run and not get weary. They will walk, and not be exhausted.   *Isaiah 40:1-2, 28-31 (HNT)*

I went to a friend's funeral today and this was one of the Scriptures that I was asked to read. Isn't that an awesome statement there in those beginning verses – my *"warfare is completed,"* and my *"iniquity is paid for"* and finally, *"from the hand of the LORD"* I will receive *"double"* for ALL my sins! WOW! What a promise! As the Bride of Christ, this is the promise! In the context of my friend's death, after battling cancer for many years, he ran the race, he kept the faith, and next is the prize for which he ran. AWESOME!

Verses 28-31 give me hope and encouragement for the race that I still have to run. God's promise is true that He does not tire in the race. He is with me every step of the way and I can rely on Him to hold me up. In fact, not just hold me up but allow me to SOAR!!! So why don't I feel like I'm soaring? Uh, maybe it's 'cause I have so many un-Godly burdens piled on my back? Why do I carry all these burdens? "If I don't – who will?" [all together now --] GOD!!! Provided they are burdens that ARE to be carried by someone! Ooops!

Another point that was made in this AWESOME worship service today is that THE most common Scripture quoted by pastors, teachers, and other Church leadership when asked a question that they do not know the answer to [like why me? Or why suffering?] is --- (drum roll, please!)

"For my thoughts are not your thoughts, and your ways are not my ways,"
declares the LORD.   *Isaiah 55:8 (HNT)*
Yes, I use it frequently, too!!!

Maybe, just maybe, the burdens that I carry are NOT meant to be carried. Maybe God is dealing with that person – or ME! – and a 'test' is being given and a GREAT testimony is going to come from it – IF I will get out of the way and let God do what God NEEDS to do!!! His 'way' has a much bigger perspective!!!

I want to soar. I want to be an eagle, not a ground hog!

Questions: What burdens do I have that really are NOT mine to carry?

Early the next morning Joshua and all the Israelites left Acacia. They traveled to the Jordan River and camped there before crossing it. After three days the officers went through the camp and gave orders to the people: "When you see the priest and Levites carrying the Ark of the Agreement with the LORD your God, leave where you are and follow it. That way you will know which way to go since you have never been here before.   *Joshua 3:1-4 (NCV)*

Here are thousands of people who have been traveling 40 years and they come to the river that is the doorway to where they want to be. The doorway to the PROMISE that God has given them. The end of a long journey is there. They can see it. And they camp THREE MORE DAYS. Why? What did they DO for three days? Were they waiting on some 'natural' phenomena like the high river to recede? Were they praying and readying themselves spiritually? I don't know but they didn't move until the ARK -- or God -- went before them and said, "COME! NOW!"

Some of us may be more likely to 'tarry' and even wait too long. Some, like me, may jump ahead and strain at the 'bit' in my mouth. Either is out of step with God. God has brought me through some discipline that has now placed my heart where He wants it -- DESIRING to be in step with Him more than myself! Now I must continue to grow in His ways so that my eyes and ears are ready to receive His timing and move accordingly. God is gracious to continue to teach me.

The LORD said, "How terrible it will be for these stubborn children. They make plans, but they don't ask me to help them. They make agreements with other nations, without asking my Spirit. They are adding more and more sins to themselves." ...

The LORD wants to show his mercy to you. He wants to rise and comfort you. The LORD is a fair God, and everyone who waits for his help will be happy.
                    Isaiah 30:1, 18 (NCV)

When I move in HIS time, there are promises He gives. I can count on that I will be WITH HIM all the way, no matter that the way may have its difficulties. Going in God's timing does NOT promise me smooth sailing.

When you pass through the waters, I will be with you. When you cross rivers, you will not drown. When you walk through fire, you will not be burned, nor will the flames hurt you. This is because I, the LORD, am your God, the Holy One of Israel, your Savior..."   *Isaiah 43:2-3 (NCV)*

It is a 'safe sanctuary' that God creates around me that assures me that He is still on the throne and NOTHING takes Him by surprise. He is with me every step of the way. He even sent Jesus, God in the flesh, to walk the same roads with the same temptations to show me the 'how' of my walk through this life. Each day is an opportunity for me to spend time with God and prepare for the journey, the plan He has for me.

Questions: How much time do I give each day for the most important research I will ever do?
Do I jump ahead or lag behind God?

I know that you sincerely trust the Lord, for you have the faith of your mother, Eunice, and your grandmother, Lois. 2 Timothy 1:5 (NLT)

I think the hardest job in the world is being a 'mom'. I know that my view might be prejudiced since I have that job. [Dads, this is for you, too!] Please notice that I said 'mom', not 'mother'. To be a 'mother' or 'father' is a biological term. If you have been given the right set of cells you can accomplish procreation. A 'mom' to me is someone who takes responsibility to teach, nurture, care, and covers it all with that indefinable wrapping called 'love'. The 'love' may be difficult to define but ask any child if they are loved by their mom and they can say "yes" or "no" rather quickly.

Being a 'mom' also covers such things like discipline and boundaries. It may mean making hard choices that forever impact your child and his/her life but the decisions are made with the conviction to do anything else in the situation will mean worse pain and destruction. It's easy to play 'Monday morning quarterback' 10-20 years later but I am convinced that any decision made with love for the child is not a WRONG decision. Hindsight brings wisdom and maybe *better* decisions in the future.

Not very long after I began my job as 'mom' in which I had had NO formal training or practice, I, like many in a new job, began to look for a manual. The shelves in any given bookstore or library is filled with people who believe they have the *FORMULA* to raise a healthy, well-adjusted child. If that were true, these writers would have received the Nobel Peace Prize by now! But there is a book that CAN BE of vital importance. Yes, the Bible.

It has become clear to me, however, that the book is not enough. What brings a child up to love God, obey God, and follow Jesus in everything that he/she does must include – EXAMPLE. It is not enough for me to TEACH my children about God. I must walk out MY life every day in front of my children. If I tell my child one thing and do another then all I have taught them is the definition of a hypocrite. Following Jesus' example both in my house and with everyone I meet: boss, co-workers, relatives, spouse, is how I pass along MY FAITH to my child and KNOW that seeds have been planted.

But when the Holy Spirit controls our lives, he will produce this kind of fruit in us: love, joy, peace, patience, kindness, goodness, faithfulness, gentleness, and self-control. Here there is no conflict with the law. Galatians 5:22-23 (NLT)
Fix your thoughts on what is true and honorable and right. Think about things that are pure and lovely and admirable, excellent and worthy of praise. Keep putting into practice all you learned from me and heard from me and saw me doing, and the God of peace will be with you. Philippians 4:8-9 (NLT)

"Whatever you have learned, received, heard, or seen in me – put into practice. If you do that, God's peace will be with you." Scary stuff! If my children, (remember, biology may have no part in those I know as 'my children') will put into practice what they have learned from me then God's peace will be a part of them. My children must learn not only about my 'victories' but also they must see my 'struggles' when God's peace is really there and making a difference. By God's grace, I am a 'mom'.

(continued from Week 24)

Questions: What are some positive things that I learned from my parents or teachers that I have or would want to pass along? Why?

An Ordinary Person

Rev. Perry Dalton – from a broken home, God brought this man out of the ashes and called him to be a pastor and an apostle to many of His children. It's not easy to be my pastor as Perry was for over ten years! God used him to harness my aggressive personality into a path of learning to trust and submit to my heavenly Father. (Notice I said, 'learning'. God is not done with me yet!) Pastoring a church that is hit with the power of God's revival is a slippery slope that is not for the faint of heart. I praise God that Perry was willing to say, "Yes" when that day came in July 1995. Because he was obedient, my children and I and literally countless others were touched by God and will never be the same again.

Two blind men were sitting beside the road and when they heard that Jesus was coming that way, they began shouting, "Sir, King David's Son, have mercy on us!" The crowd told them to be quiet, but they only yelled the louder.

When Jesus came to the place where they were he stopped in the road and called, "What do you want me to do for you?"

"Sir, they said, "we want to see!"

Jesus was moved with pity for them and touched their eyes. And instantly they could see, and followed him.   *Matthew 20:30-34 (TLB)*

What were the followers thinking??!! Two people obviously in need of a Savior and the crowd tells them to "SHUT UP!" How could any follower of Jesus keep someone from getting close to Jesus? Unfortunately, we do it a lot.

Have you ever heard someone say, "Well, I don't go to church because this church believes 'this' and another one believes 'that'. So how do I know who's right?" Or someone tells you, "Yes, I used to go to that church but when I raised some questions about why we do such-and-such…well, I got the cold shoulder after that." We spend our time scrutinizing how someone approaches Christ, making sure they 'do it right' and miss the point that Jesus just desires that they come…any way they can!

Jesus was on His way to Jerusalem. Matthew tells this story of the two blind men. Mark relates the story of the blind man, Bartimaeus. Luke remembers Jesus' parable of the ten minas and the investment that Jesus as made in us so that we may produce more 'servant fruit' to glorify the Father. John tells of another who had been in need of a Savior and wanted to express her gratitude to Jesus and so she anointed Jesus' feet and wiped them with her hair, another example of a 'ritual' that didn't meet the followers' standards but met Jesus instead!

So don't criticize each other any more. Try instead to live in such a way that you will never make your brother stumble by letting him see you doing something he thinks is wrong…In this way aim for harmony in the church and try to build each other up.   *Romans 14:13, 19 (TLB)*

Whether it is a 'brother' Christian or a 'brother' still looking for a Savior, Jesus reminds me that He was always open to those with a seeking heart. It was only the 'closed', self-centered Pharisees of the Church that He showed NO patience.

Questions: How can I clear a path to Jesus for someone today?
How does our church/fellowship 'go out' and give an invitation to come?

The woman said, "Sir, I can see that you are a prophet. My ancestors worshiped on this mountain, but you Jews say Jerusalem is the only place to worship." Jesus said to her: Believe me, the time is coming when you won't worship the Father either on this mountain or in Jerusalem. You Samaritans don't really know the one you worship. But we Jews do know the God we worship, and by using us, God will save the world. But a time is coming, and it is already here! Even now the true worshipers are being led by the Sprit to worship the Father according to the truth. These are the ones the Father is seeking to worship him." John 4:19-23 (CEV)

When my husband, Henry and I began to look for a new church to attend, it was very difficult. I had only attended two churches in my entire 40+ years. I confess that I had a preconceived notion about the church that God would send us to – what it would look like, how the worship would be, who the pastor would be as well as what his (yes, <u>his</u>) giftings would be. Whether or not the Spirit of God was in and flowing through the church would manifest itself by MY standards!

I have heard similar stories from college students, seminary students, and even an adult friend of mine who three years ago felt led to a church (and stayed) but admits that he has been 'bothered' by the fact that there was no cross as a focal point of the sanctuary. Others, including myself, have shared about the need for candles, order of worship, and even the Bible version that is read.

Jesus doesn't mention any of those things in His priorities of what 'true worship' is. He says only that we are to *"worship the Father in spirit and truth"*. Now I could rationalize that all those 'things' that I wanted could be manifestations of the Holy Spirit and God's truth. But what I hear in my spirit is – all those 'things' are <u>minors</u> and God is trying to get me to look at <u>major</u> issues. Issue. One '<u>major issue</u>' – "Jody, if I am present for you to worship and you are present worshipping <u>in</u> My Spirit and <u>in</u> My Truth, then the rest are just minor issues."

I think of Hungary (or Eastern Europe in general just a few years ago), China, and other places where Christian worship has been and still is being done in secret and in places that certainly do not LOOK like places of worship. The church that I visited my first Sunday in Hungary looks like an office building. The Communists had allowed the building to be built for a church but they got to plan and determine the architecture inside and out. The enemy used them to make the building as 'un-church-like' as he could get it. Those people didn't care! They were SO HUNGRY (no pun intended!) to worship God that they didn't care what it looked like!!!

...and they were singing the song that his servant Moses and the Lamb had sun. They were singing: "Lord God All-Powerful, you have done great and marvelous things. You are the ruler of all nations, and you do what is right and fair. Lord, who doesn't honor and praise your name? You alone are holy, and all nations will come and worship you, because you have shown that you judge with fairness." Revelation 15:3-4 (CEV)

Question: What do I 'look for' in a church? What are my 'musts'?

The Lord is the Spirit, and where the Spirit of the Lord is, there is freedom. Our faces, then, are not covered. We all show the Lord's glory, and we are being changed to be like him. This change in us brings ever greater glory, which comes from the Lord, who is the Spirit. God, with his mercy, gave us this word to do, so we don't give up. 2 Corinthians 3:17-4:1 (NCV)

That evening, Jesus said to his followers, "Let's go across the lake." Leaving the crowd behind, they took him in the boat just as he was. There were also other boats with them. A very strong wind came up on the lake. The waves came over the sides and into the boat so that it was already full of water. Jesus was at the back of the boat, sleeping with his head on a cushion. His followers woke him and said, "Teacher, don't you care that we are drowning!"

Jesus stood up and commanded the wind and said to the waves, "Quiet! Be still!" Then the wind stopped, and it became completely calm. Jesus said to his followers, "Why are you afraid? Do you still have no faith?"

The followers were very afraid and asked each other, "Who is this? Even the wind and the waves obey him!" Mark 4:35-41 (NCV)

4th of July! A day to celebrate the birth of America – freedom – and for those of us who *are* Christians, -- freedom to worship our Lord in whatever way the Holy Spirit leads us.

Oswald Chambers strikes me with the truth when he says that worry comes from wanting my own way instead of following Jesus' example. Jesus was never bothered by worry because He was not trying to accomplish His own goals but instead He was here to fulfill the Father's goals.

It would be easy for me today to look back on what God did through our forefathers and rejoice at the wars He has already brought us through.

Recently, my cousin gave me a book of family history. A genealogy "thing". I was excited to read of the faith of my – let's see – my great, great, great-grandmother and father's faith as they came from Prussia in 1847. I found out that daily morning devotions were a part of their lives. We celebrate, and others even on an international level see the freedom of our Christian faith that is the foundation of our national freedom. Mark's gospel tells me that there were 'other boats' who also must have heard Jesus' commands and were witnesses to His power in the one true God.

And so I rejoice today and pray for this nation. I receive Paul's message that God has given me this work to do and I will not worry or tire but live victoriously in Him. Let's stop right now and lift our country's leadership to the Lord and pray for God's divine guidance in all things.

Our leaders: _____

_____

_____

Week 28

William Law, a 17th century English clergyman, said, *"For there is nothing that makes us love a man so much as praying for him; and when you can once do this sincerely for any man, you have fitted your soul for the performance of everything that is kind and civil towards him."*

It's hard to be angry with someone if I am praying for them! The apostle Paul shared in the opening remarks in many of his letters about how he was praying for that particular church.

My friends, I want you to know what a hard time we had in Asia. Our sufferings were so horrible and so unbearable that death seemed certain. In fact, we felt sure that we were going to die. But this made us stop trusting in ourselves and start trusting God, who raises the dead to life. God saved us from the threat of death, and we are sure that he will do it again and again. Please help us by praying for us. Then many people will give thanks for the blessings we receive in answer to all these prayers. 2 Corinthians 1:8-11 (CEV)

I have heard about your faith in the Lord Jesus and your love for all of God's people. So I never stop being grateful for you, as I mention you in my prayers. I ask the glorious Father and God of our Lord Jesus Christ to give you his Spirit. The Spirit will make you wise and let you understand what it means to know God. My prayer is that light will flood your hearts and that you will understand the hope that was given to you when God chose you. Then you will discover the glorious blessings that will be yours together with all of God's people. I want you to know about the great and mighty power that God has for us followers.
Ephesians 1:15-19 (CEV)

I noticed that in both of these prayers Paul does not ask the Lord to make them do something. He doesn't pray a manipulative prayer. For the Corinthian church it is a prayer for thanksgiving and praise. He asks the Lord to give the Ephesian church a blessing of wisdom and revelation – GOD'S wisdom and revelation! Not his! If there is correction needed, Paul prays that God will do that.

When I come to a place where I am at odds with someone, I pray more freely when my prayer is a prayer of blessing to that person. I think prayer may need to begin and end with ME. Sounds selfish, doesn't it? But if I begin a prayer with MY praise and thanksgiving to God and asking Him to create in ME a pure heart FIRST – my spirit is ready to pray for the other person or a church or ministry with an open heart, full of the fruit of God. When I end the prayer with thanksgiving and praise that God has allowed me to lift this person and receive the blessing of watching the Lord work in this person's life or a ministry – it keeps the focus on God, giving Him all the glory for the answered prayer. As my husband says, "God answers our prayer better than we pray it!"

Questions: What is an example of a 'manipulative prayer'? How can I correct that?

[Jesus said,] *"God loved the world so much that he gave his one and only Son so that whoever believes in him may not be lost, but have eternal life. God did not send his Son into the world to judge the world guilty, but to save the world through him...They are judged by this fact: The Light has come into the world, but they did not want light. They wanted darkness, because they were doing evil things. All who do evil hate the light and will not come to the light, because it will show all the evil things they do. But those who follow the true way come to the light, and it shows that the things they do were done through God."*

John 3:16-21 (NCV)

Do you remember the day (or night) that you said, "Yes, Jesus, I need You as Savior and Lord"? Take some time today and think about it. Maybe you have been blessed to grow up always knowing about Jesus and His love and it seems He has always been there for you. But I bet there was a moment, a time, when the *enormity* of what He did for you struck a chord inside you that changed your walk with Him forever.

I don't remember a time when I didn't know the name Jesus and that He was born in a manger in Bethlehem and died on a cross on Calvary. But it took over 40 years until I admitted, accepted, the fact that Jesus did it … for me. My personal pride and at the same time my feelings of no self-worth had me rejecting the idea that Jesus did it all for me. No way! I could not accept that GOD loved me so much that He sent His Son to die for me. That I needed His Son to die for me.

My walk to freedom happened on a July night in 1995 when a preacher said, *"What good is it for a man to gain the whole world, and yet lose or forfeit his very self? If anyone is ashamed of me and my words, the Son of Man will be ashamed of him when he comes in his glory and in the glory of the Father and of the holy angels." (Luke 9:25-26 NIV, emphasis mine).* The truth ran through me like Drain-o through a clogged pipe. I was ashamed of God. I was ashamed that I needed Him and so had rejected Him ALL MY LIFE. Well...He was going to reject ME if I didn't turn around, lay that pride of mine down, and walk toward Him. It was no coincidence that I was in a room with about 2000 people. The 'ashamed factor' was going to be dealt with right then! All of this went through my mind in the three seconds after the preacher read that Scripture. I got to my feet and stepped out into the aisle and I've never looked back. My life since than has been more like the 'via dolorosa' than the 'mount of transfiguration'! It has taken me awhile to understand that walking with Christ means walking with Christ. His life here was not easy or beautiful. It was with eyes on eternity that Jesus walked this earth in peace and joy. I'm learning.

I look at my walk to Jesus and my heart is FULL and overflowing with love and gratitude for the One, the only One, who loves me, loves me without conditions and desires that I grow closer and closer to Him. My walk to freedom on that July night continues each day: "Free at last! Free at last! Thank God Almighty! I am free at last!"

Suggestion: Spend time sharing your personal 3-minute testimony.

Every king in all the earth shall give you thanks, O Lord, for all of them shall hear your voice. Yes, they shall sing about Jehovah's glorious ways, for his glory is very great. Yet though he is so great, he respects the humble, but proud men must keep their distance. Though I am surrounded by troubles, you will bring me safely through them. You will clench your fist against my angry enemies! Your power will save me. The Lord will work out his plans for my life – for your loving kindness, Lord, continues forever. Don't abandon me – for you made me.   *Psalm 138:4-8 (TLB)*

I share with you the day-to-day struggles and victories that God brings me through. I share not for sympathy. I share for two reasons: 1) Even though some may consider me a leader and a 'mature' Christian, I struggle. I desire to come closer to God <u>every</u> day. As I get closer to His holiness, there is another layer of my <u>un</u>-holiness to shed! Sometimes I gladly throw off the 'chains that bind'. Sometimes I am reluctant to give up what is familiar and comfortably uncomfortable! And 2) I need prayer from the Body of Believers. I need uplifting in prayer and there are no 'God reasons' for me not to ask! There is a Proverbs statement (27:17) about 'iron striking iron' and how we help each other with our discussions (not arguments!). We have an opportunity to build each other's faith.

...the disciples were together again, and this time Thomas was with them. The doors were locked; but suddenly, as before, Jesus was standing among them and greeting them. Then he said to Thomas, "Put your finger into my hands. Put your hand into my side. Don't be faithless any longer. Believe!"

"My Lord and my God!" Thomas said. Then Jesus told him, "You believe because you have seen me. But blessed are those who haven't seen me and believe anyway."   *John 20:26-29 (TLB)*

Jesus opens His cloak and shows me His wounds so that I may believe. I believe and follow Him because I KNOW that He has suffered and yet is faithful and obedient to God. The Son shows me the truth of the Father. I want to do the same. I want to open <u>my</u> cloak and let the world see my wounds AND see that it is <u>JESUS</u> that brings me through!

The LORD will work out his plans for my life. God is faithful and His promises are true. What a wonderful statement and promise to <u>know</u> that God already has a plan for my life and that if I keep an open heart and mind, God will show me the <u>best</u> plan for my life. I DO have a solid ROCK to stand on no matter what the storm! Struggles and victories are part of my life but traveling <u>through</u> is going to be better when I allow Jesus to be not just a 'part' but the leader and guide of my life.

Questions: What Biblical characters have been an encouragement to you? Why?

Week 31

If I must boast, I will boast of the things that show my weakness.
2 Corinthians 11:30 (ESV)

A song of ascents.
I lift up my eyes to the hills. From where does my help come from?
My help comes from the LORD who made heaven and earth..
He will not let your foot be moved; he who keeps you will not slumber.
Behold, he who keeps Israel will neither slumber nor sleep.
The LORD is your keeper; the LORD is your shade on your right hand.
The sun shall not strike you by day, nor the moon by night.
The LORD will keep you from all evil; he will keep your life;
the LORD will keep your going out and coming in from this time forth
   and forevermore. *Psalm 121 (ESV)*

"If I must 'boast', I'll boast of things that show how weak I am." Not a frequent statement of mine! In fact, I would say without hesitation – and certainly <u>not</u> bragging! – I am a person who is <u>determined</u> not to show weakness. I'm not going to varnish it – it is a CONTROL issue!!!

"I lift up my eyes – where is the help going to come from?" That usually happens as a last resort and God has frequently pulled me out of the fire! But He has also left me there! You'd think I'd learn!

"The LORD watches over" me. Cool! Then why do 'bad' things happen? Is God watching the trials and tribulations? When I get laid off my job, is God watching? When my child becomes seriously ill, is God watching? Yes. God doesn't take vacations or 'doze off'. I would not attempt to explain the mind of God but if I look at Jesus' words, it would encourage me to look beyond <u>this</u> world:

"I have said these things to you, that in me you may have peace. In the world you will have tribulation. But take heart; I have overcome the world."
John 16:33 (ESV)

I have begun to spend some 'different' kind of quiet with the Lord the last few months. As I awake in the morning and as I drift off to sleep at night, I begin to thank the Lord for the events of the day and just lay them out for Him to direct and clarify; a sort of 'before and after' view. It seems to help me come along side of <u>GOD'S</u> perspective. I am finding I <u>really</u> like that even though I continue to be puzzled by His response sometimes! Guess I haven't quite got His view yet! I want to be "*CONTENT*" in every situation and this seems to be helping me. HALLELUJAH!

I rejoiced in the Lord greatly that now at length you have revived your concern for me. You were indeed concerned for me, but you had no opportunity. Not that I am speaking of being in need, for I have learned to be content. I know how to be brought low, and I know how to abound. In any and every circumstance, I have learned the secret of facing plenty and hunger, abundance and need. I can do all things through him who strengthens me.
Philippians 4:10-13 (ESV)

Question: What are some weakness of which you can boast?

Now there was a day when the sons of God came to present themselves before the LORD, and satan also came among them. The LORD said to satan, "From where have you come?" Satan answered the LORD and said, "From going to and fro on the earth, and from walking up and down on it." And the LORD said to satan, "Have you considered my servant Job, that there is none like him on the earth, a blameless and upright man, who fears God and turns away from evil?"   *Job 1:6-8 (ESV)*

And satan then complains to God that He has set Job apart and protected him. He speculates that if God allowed Job to be 'struck' that Job would curse God.

And the LORD said to satan, "Behold, all that he has is in your hand. Only against him do not stretch out your hand." So satan went out from the presence of the LORD.   *Job 1:12 (ESV)*

Clearly, the Lord is giving satan <u>permission</u> to do what he wants with anything that Job stewards, including his family. In Job chapter 2, God gives satan permission to do what he wants with Job himself – he just can't kill him!

That can be a tough concept – satan can only do to me what God allows. When I think of some of the events in my life, I must reconcile myself that God allowed them to happen. He didn't create the cancer in my son, James, but He allowed it to happen. God didn't choose divorce for me but He allowed it to happen. Let's look at Job's reaction after all his children are dead and all his livestock and possessions are destroyed:

Then Job arose and tore his robe and shaved his head and fell on the ground and worshiped. And he said, "Naked I came from my mother's womb, and naked shall I return. The LORD gave, and the LORD has taken away; blessed be the name of the LORD." In all this Job did not sin or charge God with wrong.   *Job 1:20-22 (ESV)*

I noticed that it did not say that Job had a great revelation on <u>WHY</u> all this had happened to him. It just says that Job acknowledged that everything had come from God in the first place and was His to do with as He pleased. Job may not have understood but he trusted God. He continued to TRUST God and gave Him praise.

Now the account of Job continues with less than helpful counsel from his wife and his three friends. In fact, around chapter 38, God gets tired of 'chatter' of Job and his three friends and says:

"Who is this that darkens counsel by words without knowledge? Dress for action like a man; I will question you, and you make it known to me. Where were you when I laid the foundation of the earth? Tell me, if you have understanding."   *Job 38:2-4 (ESV)*

God clarifies to Job that He is in control of the universe and knows all things. Job may not understand why all this is happening to him but God does. (Chapters 38-42).

The account of Job ends with the Lord prospering Job again with TWICE what he had before. Does that mean that Job forgot about the children who died? I don't think so. Job received the blessings of the Lord and let the questions rest in the Lord's hands.

Week 33

Yesterday, we looked at the story of Job and how God allowed satan to strike at Job by killing all his children and destroying all that he stewarded. Let's look at how God uses satan.

First, God uses satan to refine us, the believers. I have been infected with the devil's disease: PRIDE and even in my most meek moments, I still tend to think of myself too highly. Apparently, Paul had the same problem as he shared in 2 Corinthians 12:

So that I would not become too proud of the wonderful things that were shown to me, a painful physical problem was given to me. This problem was a messenger from satan, sent to beat me and keep me from being too proud. I begged the Lord three times to take this problem away from me. But he said to me, "My grace is enough for you. When you are weak, my power is made perfect in you." So I am very happy to brag about my weaknesses. Then Christ's power can live in me.   *2 Corinthians 12:7-10 (NCV)*

While I don't know the nature of the problem, I am told plainly that it was to keep Paul humble! I am also told quite clearly that it was "*a messenger of satan*" that was to torment him AND that the messenger was under God's control. Satan was used to strengthen God's servant.

In his book, America Looks Up, Max Lucado says that satan loses even when he seems to win. As satan wields his sword and tries to give me a fatal blow, the One who is really in control causes satan's sword to in fact cut away the weeds and 'refine' those of us who faithfully believe in the Lord.

The prophet Malachi tells us that we will be refined:

No one can live through that time; no one can survive when he comes. He will be like a purifying fire and like laundry soap. Like someone who heats and purifies silver, he will purify the Levites and make them pure like gold and silver. Then they will bring offerings to the LORD in the right way. And the LORD will accept the offerings from Judah and Jerusalem, as it was in the past.
Malachi 3:2-4 (NCV)

John sees in the vision given to him that we, as the Bride of Christ, will be spotless.

Then I heard what sounded like a great many people, like the noise of flooding water, and like the noise of loud thunder. The people were saying:

"Hallelujah! Our Lord God, the Almighty, rules. Let us rejoice and be happy and give God glory, because the wedding of the Lamb has come, and the Lamb's bride has made herself ready. Fine linen, bright and clean, was given to her to wear." (The fine linen means the good things done by God's holy people.)
Revelation 19:6-8 (NCV)

The torment and trials that satan and his world lays on me can be used to refine me as I trust the Lord more and myself and my ways less.

Question: What do you think about the idea of God using satan to refine us?

How does God use even satan? Yesterday we read that God uses satan to refine the believers. God also uses satan to WAKE UP the sleeping!

When you meet together in the name of our Lord Jesus, and I meet with you in spirit with the power of our Lord Jesus, then hand this man over to satan. So his sinful self will be destroyed, and his spirit will be saved on the day of the Lord.
1 Corinthians 5:4-5 (NCV)

They knew God, but they did not give glory to God or thank him. Their thinking became useless. Their foolish minds were filled with darkness. They said they were wise, but they became fools. They traded the glory of God who lives forever for the worship of idols made to look like earthly people, birds, animals, and snakes. Because they did these things, God left them and let them go their sinful way, wanting only to do evil. As a result, they became full of sexual sin, using their bodies wrongly with each other. They traded the truth of God for a lie. They worshiped and served what had been created instead of the God who created those things, who should be praise forever. Amen.
Romans 1:21-25 (NCV)

Timothy, my child, I am giving you a command that agrees with the prophecies that were given about you in the past. I tell you this so you can follow them and fight the good fight. Continue to have faith and do what you know is right. Some people have rejected this, and their faith has been shipwrecked. Hymenaeus and Alexander have done that, and I have given them to satan so they will learn not to speak against God.
1 Timothy 1:18-20 (NCV)

These are tough words. Frankly, these are some of those Scriptures I would rather not read. *"It's not the Scriptures I don't know that bother me. It's the ones I do know!"* said Mark Twain. So now I know these Scriptures. What do I do with them? I wake up! – and ask the Holy Spirit to discuss it with me.

From Job to Paul I am told that God controls satan's actions. He 'allows' him to have input in my life. I see it as "the world" and evil. It may begin as temptation. It may be just a downright attack!

Jesus encouraged His disciples in Gethsemane to *"pray so that you will not fall into temptation" (Matthew 26:41).* He knew that satan was 'prowling' that night.

If you think you are strong, you should be careful not to fall. The only temptation that has come to you is that which everyone has. But you can trust God, who will not permit you to be tempted more than you can stand. But when you are tempted, he will also give you a way to escape so that you will be able to stand it.
1 Corinthians 10:12-13 (NCV)

Satan may tempt me but my Father has already marked out an escape path!

"So no weapon that is used against you will defeat you. You will show that those who speak against you are wrong. These are the good things my servants receive. Their victory comes from me", says the LORD. *Isaiah 54:17 (NCV)*

I may receive an attack from satan's little minions but they can NOT stand against me AND my Lord! I am awake and ready for battle!

Question: What kind of 'sneaky' attacks have you experienced?

How does God use satan? First, God uses satan to refine the believers. He also uses satan to wake up the sleeping. Finally, God uses satan to teach the Church.

[Jesus said,] *"Simon, Simon, satan has asked to test all of you as a farmer sifts his wheat. I have prayed that you will not lose your faith! Help your brothers be stronger when you come back to me."*   *Luke 22:31-32 (NCV)*

[Jesus is praying to His Father.] *I am praying for them. I am not praying for people in the world but for those you gave me, because they are yours. All I have is yours, and all you have is mine. And my glory is shone through them. I am coming to you; I will not stay in the world any longer. But they are still in the world. Holy Father, keep them safe by the power of your name, the name you gave me, so they may be one, just as you and I are one."*

         John 17:9-11 (NCV)

Isn't it awesome that Jesus <u>knew</u> us even 2000 years ago and spoke to the Father about us. He prayed and interceded for us then and He continues to do so now. We have God's strength to get through the 'sifting'. I told a group at a conference that Jesus is coming back for His BRIDE – not a girlfriend! We as a Church must see ourselves as THE BRIDE – and as a bride, desire to be SO BEAUTIFUL before our Groom. A bride does not come to her wedding without combing her hair or taking a shower! The dress that a bride wears isn't dirty with mud from a recent run through a field. It won't have old stains from 'unimportant' past games. A bride is as beautiful as she can be and will do whatever it takes to be a 'vision' of loveliness. That means – acknowledging our sin, repenting, accepting God's freely given mercy, and turning towards holiness, which is where HIS strength comes in.

[Joseph said to his brothers,] *"You meant to hurt me, but God turned your evil into good to save the lives of many people, which is being done."*

         Genesis 50:20 (NCV)

God is SO GLORIFIED and satan is SO FRUSTRATED through these times!

I remember when my oldest son was around 18 mos. old and I was baking 'something' in the oven. He kept 'toddling' over and wanting to touch the oven door. I told him "NO!" and slapped his little hand with a "NO!" but he stood there, waiting for a chance to touch it any way. I knew it wouldn't <u>burn</u> him but I also knew it would hurt. I finally turned my back – and there he went. "Waaaa!!!" He had finally gotten what he wanted and it HURT! He looked up at me with those big blue eyes full of tears like "Mama, how could you let that happen?!" He never touched a hot stove again. God 'allows' me to learn because He loves me SO much.

The Father has loved us so much that we are called children of God. And we really are his children. The reason the people in the world do not know us is that they have not known him.   *1 John 3:1 (NCV)*

Questions: In what ways has the Father loved you this week?
Does it bring a different perspective when trials and suffering come?
Remember that God gave us the Holy Spirit and other believers to hold us up!

God, I look to you for help. I trust in you, LORD. Don't let me die. Protect me from the traps they set for me and from the net that evil people have spread. Let the wicked fall into their own nets, but let me pass by safely.

Psalm 141:8-10 (NCV)

James B. Crooks said, "A man who wants to lead the orchestra must turn his back on the crowd." Wise words. I believe this is the pit that most of us in Church leadership fall and then wonder how we got there. It is a pit that is full of those who are anxious to criticize EVERYTHING and yet do little or NOTHING themselves when the 'call' comes to work outside the USUAL.

Jesus worked outside – the usual. Jesus healed on the Sabbath (even in the Temple) and THAT was a DIFFERENT Sabbath service. Jesus allowed His disciples to glean grain from a field on the Sabbath and THAT was considered UNNECESSARY work. Jesus told the Church to pay the taxes to Caesar (even if they were unfair) and THAT was when the leadership WANTED Him to be RADICAL and He was not!

Don't depend on your own wisdom. Respect the LORD and refuse to do wrong. Then your body will be healthy, and your bones will be strong.

Proverbs 3:7-8 (NCV)

I am very familiar with verse 6 of this Proverb that tells me to trust in God and not in my own understanding and yet I miss the second part of the admonition and continue to try to 'reason out' my walk with God instead of letting go of my own wisdom and accepting that God is God and walk on His path, away from evil and confusion, letting God direct the path with HIS ALL-KNOWING eyes.

Paul and those with him went through the areas of Phrygia and Galatia since the Holy Spirit did not let them preach the Good News in the country of Asia. When they came near the country of Mysia, they tried to go into Bithynia, but the Spirit of Jesus did not let them. So they passed by Mysia and went to Troas. That night Paul saw in a vision a man from Macedonia. The stood and begged, "Come over to Macedonia and help us." After Paul had seen the vision, we immediately prepared to leave for Macedonia, understanding that God had called us to tell the Good News to those people. Acts 16:6-10 (NCV)

I've never heard a sermon on this passage. I wonder why. Paul, a smart man, schooled in the languages and spiritual wisdom of his time, changes his evangelism plan because *"the Spirit of Jesus would not allow them"* to enter a region. They went to a different city. And then, 24 hours later, Paul has a vision and goes to yet another place. His ministry is directed and redirected by the Spirit of God. Now, I bet the Holy Spirit also gave Paul some long-range visions also. But the point would be that Paul went with whatever was on GOD'S plan for today or next year, not what statistics dictated. Did Paul have people who were what I would call 'accountability brothers'? I don't know. It doesn't say that specifically but there were some notes in Acts and in his letters where Paul speaks of the concept of accountability and if Paul was teaching that I make the assumption that he also lived it. As I should live what I teach!

Hand to the plow. Eyes on Jesus. Moving ahead. Let the dogs bark – but the train moves on. THAT is God's way.

(continued from Week 36)

Suggestion: Share any times in your life when you felt God direct you to do something specific that seemed 'strange' at the time (call someone or pray).
OR
Look at some of the stories in the Bible (Noah, Jacob) where God directed people to 'do' and may or may not have told them why.

An Ordinary Person

Laney Beard – born in rural Florida in a strong family of faith, Laney grew up in the middle of a sister and three brothers. She has had many different and powerful experiences within the Body of Christ that have given her unique knowledge of how churches fulfill their 'call' with Christ's Church. When I began to pray for an 'accountability sister', I pictured us sitting at a table with a tea pot between us and our Bibles open. I knew that our time together would be uplifting and joyous! God sent me a 'sister' that would hold my feet to the fire because He desired that I grow up and leave behind my selfish desires and ambitions. He sent Laney to me who looks at me with love and compassion and tells me the truth, straight from the Father's heart. I praise God for all the tears and laughter that we have shared and look forward to what God is going to do next in our lives.

Week 37

Blessed is the one whose transgression is forgiven, whose sin is covered. Blessed is the man against whom the LORD counts no iniquity, and in whose spirit there is no deceit.   *Psalm 32:1-2 (ESV)*

David tells us — he confessed — and God forgave him. A done deal. But let's look at another story in 1 Samuel 15:

* King Saul is told by the prophet Samuel that the LORD wants him to go WIPE OUT the Amalekites for what they had done to Israel. v.3 *"Now go, attack the Amalekites and totally destroy everything that belongs to them. Do not spare them; put to death men and women, children and infants, cattle and sheep, camels and donkeys.' "*

* So Saul takes 210,000 men and attacks. BUT —v. 8 *"Saul and the army spared Agag (the king) and the best of the sheep and cattle, the fat calves and lambs--everything that was good. These they were unwilling to destroy completely, but everything that was despised and weak they totally destroyed."*

* And what was God's response to that? v. 11-12 *"I am grieved that I have made Saul king, because he has turned away from me and has not carried out my instructions." Samuel was troubled, and he cried out to the LORD all that night. Samuel interceded for his disobedient king. The next morning, he got up and went to look for him.*

* v.13 *When Samuel reached him, Saul said, "The LORD bless you! I have carried out the LORD's instructions."* LIAR!

* Saul goes on to add lie after lie on top of his disobedience! EXCUSES, EXCUSES, EXCUSES!!!

* Finally Samuel says, "STOP!" He tells Saul what the Lord told him during the night — the <u>truth</u> of what Saul had done.

* Saul <u>again</u> makes excuses and tries to weasel around make it sound like he <u>had</u> obeyed the Lord — technically — like he <u>knew</u> the Lord would not want him to kill the 'good stuff'!!!

* Samuel cuts to the bottom line and says, *"Has the LORD as great delight in burnt offerings and sacrifices, as in obeying the voice of the LORD? Behold, to obey is better than sacrifice, and to listen than the fat of rams. For rebellion is as the sin of divination, and presumption is as iniquity and idolatry. Because you have rejected the word of the LORD, he has also rejected you from being the king."*   *vv.22-23*

And that was it for Saul. I don't believe that God was harsh because Saul was disobedient — it was because Saul refused to repent — turn away and admit he had disobeyed.

Mercy by definition is undeserved forgiveness. Every sin I commit requires God's forgiveness. Any attempt to defend myself is worthless and is a mockery to God. When I first feel the conviction, may I fall on my face at the feet of our Savior, confess my sin and plead His great mercy --- and <u>receive it</u>! He does not hold it back when I humble myself and ask!

Suggestion: Sometimes repentance for a repeating sin or a sin that we have found difficult to forgive <u>ourselves</u> produces *victory* when we have witnesses.

Then the LORD said to Noah, "Go into the ark, you and all your household, for I have seen that you are righteous before me in this generation...For in seven days I will send rain on the earth forty days and forty nights, and every living thing that I have made I will blot out from the face of the ground." And Noah did all that the LORD commanded him...In the six hundredth year of Noah's life, in the second month, on the seventeenth day of the month, on that day all the fountains of the great deep burst forth, and the windows of the heavens were opened. And rain fell upon the earth forty days and forty nights.

Genesis 7:1,4-5, 11-12 (ESV)

I believe that this really happened. I believe Noah and his wife and sons and daughters-in-law were ridiculed by everyone they knew for building this huge boat. And then the rain came. And came. And came. And the boat began to float. And the cries outside the boat began as people realized that the water was going to continue to rise and the rain was going to continue to fall. Aunts, uncles, cousins, friends – all crying outside the boat "Help!" "Noah!" "Jehovah, help us!" But it was too late.

The apostle, Paul, someone who KNEW the law, also knew we could NOT obtain our eternal salvation by obedience to the law and the works of our own hands.

For by grace you have been saved through faith. And this is not your own doing; it is the gift of God, not a result of works, so that no one may boast. For we are his workmanship, created in Christ Jesus for good works, which God prepared beforehand, that we should walk in them. *Ephesians 2:8-10 (ESV)*

Scripture tells us that *"Noah was a righteous man, blameless among the people of his time, and he walked with God."* *Genesis 6:9* It doesn't say this inclusively, extending to his wife, sons, and their wives. It seems to imply that they came under Noah's 'umbrella'. If that is so, I wonder what went through their minds as they sat inside this boat hearing the cries of those outside and remembering their own moments of unrighteousness. A reminder to <u>me</u> that *"It is by grace you have been saved."*

I do not know what it is going to be like in the times ahead. There's the rapture where I could be in line at Wal-Mart and then GONE! Will the woman and her 12-year-old son in front of me stay? There's Judgment Day where Jesus calls me as a 'sheep' to come join Him at the wedding feast. Will I notice the 'goats' walking the other way?

Now is the time for me to realize that I have been called to be a part of the 'Heaven Bound Tours'. There may be many who are watching, silently wondering about this huge boat that GOD has built. (HE built it—it's that 'grace thing'!) There may be some who are openly critical and down right UGLY about the invitation! There may be many who are 'clue-less' and seemingly do not care. While God builds the boat, He has sent me to invite others to come. He really doesn't want anyone crying outside after the door is shut. **What excuse do I have today for not sharing about this 'grace thing'?**

About the middle of the feast Jesus went up into the temple and began teaching. The Jews therefore marveled, saying, "How is it that this man has learning, when he has never studied?" So Jesus answered them, "My teaching is not mine, but his who sent me. If anyone's will is to do God's will, he will know whether the teaching is from God or whether I am speaking on my own authority. The one who speaks on his own authority seeks his own glory, but the one who seeks the glory of him who sent him is true, and in him there is no falsehood." John 7:14-18 (ESV)

Teach me your way, O LORD, that I may walk in your truth; unite my heart to fear your name. I give thanks to you, O Lord my God, with my whole heart, and I will glorify your name forever. For great is your steadfast love toward me; you have delivered my soul from the depths of Sheol. Psalm 86:11-13 (ESV)

When our children would have their first tests of a new school year, they would say that those were the 'good' kind because they were essentially reviewing information from last year. No new concepts.

Even though at my "extreme age" I haven't taken a test since Flo Nightingale and I were in school together (!), but I remember the feelings like it was yesterday. Some tests were 'good' in that I went in feeling confident and prepared for the test and expected to do well. Most were tests that I studied and went in 'wired' but feeling prepared. A few (fortunately only a <u>few</u>) were tests that caused sweaty palms and an increased heart rate because I did not study and I was not prepared! And then one stands out in a class by itself (NURSING BOARDS!!!) — I had studied all through college and 'crammed' for the first time in my life — and <u>still</u> I was sweaty and nervous.

Life has its tests. I don't think I am exaggerating by saying — <u>DAILY</u> tests. Have I studied? Am I prepared? Studying requires: 1) the right resources/teachers — The Bible (the standard for all others) and the One who inspired it, other authors, church leadership and brothers and sisters in the Lord 2) the right environment to study — worship, my private devotion time, study groups and 3) my attitude and desire to grow and learn.

Being prepared begins with knowing that there will be tests. I don't know if I had my first test in first grade or if it was second grade. I just remember being so taken by surprise and — PANICKED! — and — so out of control! Now I know that all that analysis comes from an adult looking back on a childhood memory — but I can certainly see parallel truths in my adult life.

Yes, life has its tests and I need to be prepared DAILY for these tests. I need to do <u>my</u> part in daily study and then plant my feet FIRMLY on the other part — that GOD is there and has in fact already gone before me! Big or small — I will never take another test alone. Some may be 'pop' tests — some may be 'end of the semester' EXAMS — but I am not alone.

What is the 'test' today? OK, God, let's go do it! Lord, I want to glorify You!

Suggestion: List some 'tests' that come your way.
What does God say about them?

Never stop praying, especially for others. Always pray by the power of the Spirit. Stay alert and keep praying for God's people.   Ephesians 6:18 (CEV)

There have been difficult times in my life. Looking back, I can see the 'season' of difficulty had a beginning and end and between there were wonderful messengers of God who encouraged me to keep going – I could make it to the end of the current race! Right now, this season is the most difficult that I could ever had imagined. The life-threatening illness of my son is a journey we have been on for several years now but our current 'season' appears to be the most difficult as I watch my child walk through a journey I never thought I would see and that he wouldn't take for another 60 years.

Many people want to do something. I have heard more about various health-promoting diets and various vitamin and minerals supplements than I knew existed or learned about in nursing school.

It is those people who send me a note or touch my hand or arm and say, "I pray for your son every day" that brings encouragement and keeps my eyes on the Hope that we have in Jesus. As one that has been in the medical profession 'way too many years, I know just how little that it is about pills and procedures and how much it is about prayer and God!

"Never stop praying". *"Always pray by the power of the Spirit"*. It seems that every prayer would be under Holy Spirit guidance. I had a friend come to me just the other day and say, "I was praying for you and 'felt led' to pray, not for you at that time but for your doctor. I don't know who he is but I prayed for 15 minutes just about him." She didn't know that we had a meeting with him that day and it was wonderful the way he spoke to my son and encouraged him. Praying with the Holy Spirit means prayers may take a path that wasn't in my plan but was known by God to be accurate and perfect!

So the sisters sent word to Jesus, "Lord, the one you love is sick."   John 11:3

This comes from the story of Lazarus. We aren't told who the messenger is but he must have been someone that the sisters really trusted to get the message through and convey it with the right tone of urgency and importance. A petition, a prayer is sent to Jesus about a need. The prayer reminds Jesus that it is not about "…the one who loves You, Lord" but rather it is about *"the one you love is sick"*. God hears and answers prayers out of HIS great love, not mine. God hears and answers prayers out of HIS great love.

And so today, I am encouraged and comforted to know that many people are helping today – they are praying. And I am encouraged and comforted to know that GOD hears and answers my prayers and their prayers because of HIS love. I have ALL I need.

[Author note: James died September 22, 2004 at the age of 17.]

Questions: Do you have a prayer chain at your church? Are you a part of it? Why or why not?

Their work won't be wasted, and their children won't die of dreadful diseases.
I will bless their children and their grandchildren.
I will answer their prayers before they finish praying.   Isaiah 65:23-24 (CEV)

"Sometimes I wonder if God hears me." "Sometimes I wonder if He cares." These are not unusual thoughts when going through troubled times. How do I really know God is concerned about me and my problems? How does my concern for my son who is far away from home stack up against a major war and famine to my Heavenly Father?

God told us through Isaiah that even before I 'call' to Him – He answers. While I am still 'splaining things to Him – He hears. God is not constrained by multiple cries for help nor does He have 'off' hours when He takes vacation or sleeps. Isaiah testified himself that:

Don't you know? Haven't you heard?
The LORD is the eternal God, Creator of the earth.
He never gets weary or tired; his wisdom cannot be measured.
The LORD gives strength to those who are weary.
Even young people get tired, then stumble and fall.   Isaiah 40:28-30 (CEV)

The night He died, Jesus prayed for us. The Son of God, in the moments when He was about to begin the final walk of His life here on earth, when He was about to complete the mission that He had been given to do – prayed for me.

"I am not praying just for these followers. I am also praying for everyone else, who will have faith because of what my followers will say about me. I want all of them to be one with each other, just as I am one with you and you are one with me. I also want them to be one with us. Then the people of this world will believe that you sent me...I told them what you are like, and I will tell them even more. Then the love that you have for me will become part of them, and I will be one with them."   John 17:20-21, 26 (CEV)

Jesus prays for me that I will not only be united with ALL who call themselves believers in Him but that I will be completely united with HIM.

Stormie Omartian shared in her recent book, *Praying Through Life's Problems,* that she had walked with the Lord for 32 years and more time she spent with Him the less discouragement and fear she experienced when troubles occurred. She found she hung on to God's hope, knowing that He was in control. Continuous prayer keeps her in close touch with her Lord, remembering that she cannot live without Him and so He needs to be in charge of her life.

I give my burdens to Jesus because He DOES care for me.

Questions: What burdens do I have today?
What specific ways do I lay those burdens down or give them to Jesus each day?

Week 42

"Come to me, all who labor and are heavy laden, and I will give you rest."
Matthew 11:29 (ESV)

Jesus' words are recorded as He walks the many miles encouraging the people to repent and turn their hearts to God. He has just given His "woe" rebuke, telling the people that miracles have been performed in their midst and yet they continue to harden their hearts and not repent. It seems like the righteous anger leaves Jesus and He tries once again to meet the people with compassion, affirming that He sees their hardship and invites them to come to Him where they will find true rest.

The Spirit and the Bride say, "Come." And let the one who hears say, "Come." And let the one who is thirsty come; let the one who desires take the water of life without price.
Revelation 22:17 (ESV)

From Old Testament to New we are invited to refresh ourselves in the "living water" that comes from God. Psalms and Proverbs tell us of streams of refreshing that only God can give. Jesus told the Samaritan woman that if she drank from the "living water" that she would never be thirsty again. Jesus exhorted the people in John chapter 7 that if we would believe in Him, "streams of living water will flow from within" us, meaning the Holy Spirit.

Our days here on this earth seem to be increasingly filled with suffering from disease and war and atrocities that humans commit against one another. Self-help books and hours of talk shows on relationships are not going to alleviate the pain. Only through mighty God, Jehovah, the Alpha and Omega, the One who has always been and will always be – can I find 'rest' and a quenching of the thirst that has not end. Looking in any other place will only bring more disappointment and frustration in my life as I attempt to find 'rest' in distractions that produce no solutions and a 'quenching' in substances that only demand that I drink more!

Is God too abstract, too nebulous like a cloud that blows across my life? No. God is real and tangible when I reach out and turn towards Him. It's just a step. It's just an admission: "Lord, I've looked everywhere and found nothing that I can count on. I'm sorry that I turned to You last. I need You. Come into my life and be my Lord and Savior."

God told Joshua, *"No man shall be able to stand before you all the days of your life. Just as I was with Moses, so I will be with you. I will not leave you or forsake you."*
Joshua 1:5 (ESV)

David said in Psalm 27, *"For my father and my mother have forsaken me, but the LORD will take me in."*
Psalm 27:10 (ESV)

The writer of Hebrews repeats God's words to Moses from Deuteronomy 31, *"I will never leave you nor forsake you."* and goes on to say, *"So we can confidently say, 'The Lord is my helper; I will not fear; what can man do to me?"*
Hebrews 13:5-6 (ESV)

Though you have not seen him, you love him. Though you do not now see him, you believe in him and rejoice with joy that is inexpressible and filled with glory, obtaining the outcome of your faith, the salvation of your souls.
1 Peter 1:8-9 (ESV)

(continued from Week 42)

Questions: How does God refresh you?

An Ordinary Person

Marybelle Grossheider was third generation American, growing up during the post-war depression in the 'heartland' of the United States. She thought of herself as a farm girl and was proud of the work ethic that she had learned from her parents who, though very poor, always had 'some to share'. As the oldest of five children, she was given adult responsibilities early in life and was able to only complete the eighth grade.

She grew up with a strong faith that was walked out in the every day life of her family. Though they never considered themselves 'poor like other people', food came from what they raised on the farm and clothing was self-made and handed down. God was a central figure in the home and recognized as the One who had provided all that they needed.

She married a man who was raised in a different denomination in a time when this was not often done. She was not even allowed to be married inside the church but instead they were married in the pastor's house. My brother and I were raised in Mother's faith but we went to both churches for Christmas and Easter. We were taught that we all believed in Jesus Christ as Savior and Lord but that we were traveling slightly different roads in the same direction to live eternally with Jesus.

One of my earliest memories of my mother was seeing her sitting on the side of her bed, praying. Later, she would sit in a chair beside the bed, morning and night, quietly and fervently praying. Whenever some 'bad news' would come, I would find Mother sitting in her chair or out in the garden or down in the basement washing clothes, her mouth whispering prayers.

Late in her life, her mind weakened by multiple strokes and frequent confusion, making it impossible for her to live alone, she still found peace when she was taken to prayer services. All my life, Mom showed me the peace that could be found when I sought the presence of God in prayer. She was just an ordinary farm girl used by an extra-ordinary God.

So that I would not become too proud of the wonderful things that were shown to me, a painful physical problem was given to me. This problem was a messenger from Satan, sent to beat me and keep me from being too proud. I begged the Lord three times to take this problem away from me. But he said to me, "My grace is enough for you. When you are weak, my power is made perfect in you." So I am happy to brag about my weaknesses. Then Christ's power can live in me. For this reason I am happy when I have weaknesses, insults, hard times, sufferings, and all kinds of trouble for Christ. Because when I am weak, then I am truly strong.　　　　　　　　　　　　　*2 Corinthians 12:7-10 (NCV)*

I grew up in the Midwest and learned about tornadoes. Now I've lived in Florida for over 20 years. I've learned a lot about hurricanes. A wind blowing at over 120 mph can drive a pinecone through my windshield or a pine <u>needle</u> into the trunk of a tree like it was an arrow! It's all about force.

'Grace' is about power but it's not about force. I don't think I can <u>receive</u> God's grace unless I want it. Grace is unconditional love. There is much speculation about this 'thorn' that Paul speaks about. It could be a physical condition or it could be a person or situation. Paul says he <u>pleaded</u> with God to remove the torment. He didn't <u>ask</u> – he PLEADED! God responded that <u>HIS</u> unconditional love was enough. ENOUGH – SUFFICIENT!!! ALL that Paul needed! If grace was what Paul needed, maybe the 'thorn' was a person or a situation involving a person or group of people. God says His 'unconditional love' was enough but would Paul be weak enough – OPEN ENOUGH – to let God's <u>unconditional</u> love fill him up so that he could <u>receive</u> the POWER of Christ's unconditional love. His 'grace'.

But God's mercy is great, and he loved us very much. Though we were spiritually dead because of the things we did against God, he gave us new life with Christ. You have been saved by God's grace.　　　　*Ephesians 2:4-5 (NCV)*

I was 'saved' because I was weak and so lost, having no where else to go and opened myself to receive only what God could *give* me – LIFE – ETERNAL LIFE! God could not *force* that unconditional love on me. I had to open the door and say, "YES! I want it!" So easy – yet, so hard, because it has nothing – NOTHING – to do with any worthiness or strength within me – it's about being too weak to do anything else!

Since we have a great high priest, Jesus the Son of God, who has gone into heaven, let us hold on to the faith we have. For our high priest is able to understand our weaknesses. When he lived on earth, he was tempted in every way that we are, but he did not sin. Let us, then, feel very sure that we can come before God's throne where there is grace. There we can receive mercy and grace to help us when we need it.　　　　　　　　　　*Hebrews 4:14-16 (NCV)*

The *power* of grace comes straight from the throne room of God. It is not a *little* gift or a *cheap* gift. I believe it is a gift of POWER that works MIRACULOUSLY every time! I open my arms WIDE because I need a lot of 'grace' <u>today</u>!

Suggestion: Share how God's grace has specifically touched you.

Here are two gospel stories about healing and faith:

Later Jesus went to Jerusalem for a special Jewish feast. In Jerusalem there is a pool with five covered porches, which is called Bethzatha in the Jewish language. This pool is near the Sheep Gate. Many sick people were lying on the porches beside the pool. Some were blind, some were crippled, and some were paralyzed. A man was lying there who had been sick for thirty-eight years.

John 5:1-5 (NCV)

When Jesus was leaving there, two blind men followed him. They cried out, "Have mercy on us, Son of David!" After Jesus went inside, the blind men went with him. He asked the men, "Do you believe that I can make you see again?" They answered, "Yes, Lord." Then Jesus touched their eyes and said, "Because you believe I can make you see again, it will happen." Then the men were able to see. But Jesus warned them strongly, saying, "Don't tell anyone about this."

Matthew 9:27-30 (NCV)

Faith. Does God answer prayer according to <u>our faith</u>? Is the <u>will</u> of the Almighty contingent upon what I believe and how much I believe about Him?

Faith means being sure of the things we hope for and knowing that something is real even if we do not see it. Faith is the reason we remember great people who lived in the past. *Hebrews 11:1 (NCV)*

One of the most well-known verses in the Bible about faith. The next 36 verses tell us about these wonderful 'great people' and their faith, implying that they were extra-ordinary, void of doubt. Hmmmm.

Abel – well, he ends up murdered.

Abraham – let's see: he lied to a king about his wife, he doubted God and manipulated His promise, causing a whole mess of problems with the begetting of Ishmael <u>and</u> Isaac, <u>and</u> he dodged the bullet in sacrificing Isaac.

Jacob – manipulated his brother, his father and lived most of his adult years in exile

Joseph – sold as a slave, is wrongfully accused of adultery, and ends up in prison and then becomes #2 man in Egypt – then manipulates <u>his</u> brothers out of revenge

Moses – whined his way through his 'call' from God until God's anger 'burned' against him

Israelites – whined and complained for 40 years on a trip that should have been done in a couple of weeks

The walls of Jericho – fell down because of <u>Joshua's</u> obedience to God and the people's love and obedience to <u>Joshua</u> it seems to me, not God.

We have around us many people whose lives tell us what faith means. SO let us run the race that is before us and never give up...Let us look only to Jesus, the One who began our faith and who makes it perfect. *Hebrews 12:1-2 (NCV)*

And, for me, here is the answer to my original question. It is not <u>my</u> faith that is counted when I petition God. It is my complete weakness in Jesus. I come to God asking for healing and mercy and help, stinky in my sins, and Jesus steps in front of me so that all the Father sees is a beautiful daughter with a request.

Suggestion: Pray and believe in God's mercy and love for _____.

Hallelujah! Thank you, Lord! How good you are! Your love for me continues on forever. Who can ever list the glorious miracles of God? Who can ever praise him half enough? Happiness comes to those who are fair to others and are always just and good.   *Psalm 106:1-3 (TLB)*

Don't let evil get the upper hand but conquer evil by doing good.

Obey the government, for God is the one who has put it there. There is no government anywhere that God has not placed in power. So those who refuse to obey the laws of the land are refusing to obey God, and punishment will follow.   *Romans 12:21-13:2 (TLB)*

Remind your people to obey the government and its officers, and always to be obedient and ready for any honest work. They must not speak evil of anyone, nor quarrel, but be gentle and truly courteous to all.   *Titus 3:1-2 (TLB)*

We are truly blessed to have an opportunity to exercise our right <u>AND</u> responsibility to vote. When I first began to vote my decisions on which candidate or on the resolutions were based on whatever my friends said or what my parents said (sometimes I would vote opposite of my parents, after all what did <u>they</u> know?!) or who was cute or charismatic. Good reasoning, huh?!

Now almost 30 years later, I would have to testify that <u>PRAYER</u> is the ONLY way to know God's will and His knowledge of the true hearts of those who are running or the truth of the resolutions. It is unfortunate that mentioning religious beliefs has become a plus in getting votes whether it is the truth or not. It is also true that a candidate may have some views that are different than mine but his/her heart is truly seeking God's will and maybe we <u>both</u> have something to learn from that!

I will pray each time that I go to the voting booth for God's wisdom. I ask that He confirm to me His will regardless of the candidate's party affiliation. I ask that I read clearly the resolutions and issues that are before me, seeing with God's eyes and heart.

Let us also remember to pray each day for our President and leadership, not that they do MY will but that they do GOD'S will and be obedient and answerable to the Lord. May they be blessed with God's wisdom, strength, and understanding that is far greater than man's. May the leaders of our country and city look for Godly solutions. Praying blessings on our government leaders and officials is certainly something they will be grateful to receive!

Jesus told us to 'give to the government what is the government's and to God the things that are God's'. Good advice.

Question: How do you decide who to vote for?
What is the most important 'point' that figures into your decision? Is it: personality, issues, integrity, beliefs/faith, or something else?

...Respect the LORD your God, and do what he has told you to do. Love him. Serve the LORD your God with your whole being, and obey the LORD's commands and laws that I am giving you today... Deuteronomy 10:12-13 (NCV)

Before I made a decision to let go and turn my life over to God, I allowed it to be SO complicated. It's NOT complicated. It's just not EASY! It is very different than this 'microwave' world I live in. When you eat good ol' white Irish potatoes, do you fix the *instant* kind? Or do you buy the ones in a 5 or 10 lb. sack, take them home and wash them, stand at the sink and peel them, chop them up, stick them in a pot with water and salt, and boil them for about 15 minutes or so, mash them adding milk and butter, then mix them on high with your electric mixer (that you had to take out and dust off!) until they are fluffy with maybe juuuuuust a few little lumps in them so you know they're the 'real McCoy' and then finish them off with just a little pat of butter so it melts and drips down that mountain of potatoes? Makes you want to sneer at the *instant* ones, doesn't it? Making *real* mashed potatoes isn't complicated; it just takes some time and effort! Accepting God for who He is and His Son as Savior and Lord, isn't complicated, it just takes some time and effort!

Moses speaks clearly to us about what the Lord asks of me in this relationship:

- Fear Him. This is a Holy fear, not a 'BOO!' in the dark fear. This isn't about 'when is God going to whack me up side of the head because of what I've done'. This is about grabbing on to the <u>fact</u> that He is Lord, Creator of ALL the universe and HE wants to be in *close* relationship to ME!!!

- Walk in all his ways – be obedient – observe what He tells me to do. Again, not complicated, just takes some time and effort to learn and build a relationship with God that brings forth <u>love</u> that *inspires* me to be obedient. Yes, Holy fear also helps me to be obedient when faced with choices in my life.

- Love him -- It's a relationship thing. It's reading about Him, talking to Him (and being <u>totally</u> honest), and WORSHIPPING Him for who He is. I learn more and more about that as our relationship grows!

- Serve him – In some ways, maybe that is the more difficult. God may ask me to serve in ways that are difficult for me to do. Serving Him requires me to do all the other three things and give God all the credit for it! He may ask me to serve by being quiet and in prayer when I'd rather take <u>ACTION</u>! He may ask me to GO some place that I never considered!

You adulterous people, don't you know that friendship with the world is hatred toward God? Anyone who chooses to be a friend of the world becomes an enemy of God. James 4:4

James calls us 'adulterous people' because we love someone besides the One that we are committed to – married to – are in covenant with – GOD. We find our relationship with the Lord difficult because we are full of PRIDE and IDOLIZE things other than God. And so I am back to simple – a simple choice – to be faithful to God only, to put Him FIRST in my life.

Suggestion: List the top 3 priorities in your life. Does your life reflect that?

Week 47

I would like to spend a moment, just one-to-one with each of you. And before you ask, "How can you think that you are talking just to me, Jody? You don't even know me!" No, I don't but God does. And that is really the point of His Words, isn't it? God speaks to each one of us...everyday. The devotions that we share together...it is God's words for me that day. They were not words spoken to me for Jane Smith. They were for me. When I dismiss God's words as only given for someone else, that is the very time that He will bring them back around to me again and again because I missed the point, didn't I? Here is an example: God spoke to Jonah about 3000 years ago. He brought it around to me again last night.

Now the word of the LORD came to Jonah the son of Amittai, saying, "Arise, go to Nineveh, that great city, and call out against it, for their evil has come up before me."   *Jonah 1:1-2 (ESV)*

The Assyrians were a nasty group of folks. They were pagans. They liked to do human sacrifices, including children. They were disgusting! And God sent one of His prophets to call them to repentance. He sent Jonah.

We may know the Sunday School story of how Jonah was not in agreement with God's plan and had a 'change of heart' in the belly of a whale. I did not know the history behind it and so did not really appreciate the why of Jonah's refusal to go to Nineveh. Some would say that was irrelevant and that Jonah was just disobedient, end of story. That's true but it speaks to me when I feel I have 'reasons' for arguing with God about what He is saying to me. Jonah and his people had been treated badly...more than badly...by the Assyrians. The fact that they would 'rot in hell' one day was maybe a comforting thought while Jonah and his people were being persecuted by them! Call these blood-suckers to repentance??!! Pshaw!

Jonah was finally obedient because God was rather insistent! And what do you know? The king of Assyria and all the people heard the voice of God...and repented. But Jonah got angry that the people of Nineveh did not get punished!

GET OVER IT, JODY, (I mean) JONAH! The story of Jonah isn't just about a whale and how God used it to change a prophet's mind to be obedient! The lesson doesn't stop when the whale burps him out on the shore! Jonah still didn't get it!

When God tells me to go, that's the first step. I am to be obedient to that. When God tells me that I've done what I was supposed to do, places His hand on me in blessing, I am to rejoice! I do not 'tweak' the situation a bit more or tell God how to improve or finish the project! I am part of God's Body through Jesus Christ. I am part. Like Jonah, I may find that difficult because the people He calls me to minister may not show me what I want to see happen. I may not think they repent enough! I may think they got 'off' too lightly! GET OVER IT, JODY! YOU'RE NOT ME (GOD)!!! God has the situation under control. He gives me a job for a season. I am obedient to that and move on and rejoice over what has been whether I saw the outcome I expected or not. I don't want to get stuck looking back but instead to look forward to what God will do next!

Question: What 'word' has God brought up to you lately with a lesson?

Week 48

And their hearing was immediately opened up, and the bonds of their tongues were broken, and they spoke clearly. And Jesus commanded them not to tell anyone, but the more he commanded the more they proclaimed. And the crowd was amazed beyond all measure and said, "He has done everything well, and he makes the deaf hear and the dumb speak." Mark 7:35-37 (HNT)

Do you find something every day that you would term 'amazing'? It occurred to me this morning that I may have become a little jaded in my 21st century thinking. My mind quickly flips through my folders of knowledge and attempts to explain most of the things that come to my eyes' attention. There are not many occasions that I am stopped with a stunning blow of 'amazement'. That is unfortunate because there are still many amazing things in my life.

I took a trip this past week in my van to visit my son and his family. It was amazing that I drove about 150 miles on a highway with thousands of other vehicles and reached my destination safely in about two hours. When my parents were the age of my children, the same trip would have been done in a vehicle that would have taken six hours. Amazing.

I go into my living room and turn on a screen that gives me pictures of events and people around the world. I receive information from my television minutes after it happens. I can send a message through my computer to someone thousands of miles around the world from me and they will receive it in minutes. I can listen to my son play a baseball game through my computer. Amazing.

I look at my children and see myself or their father and yet they are individuals with physical and emotional characteristics all their own. I can look at my grandchildren and see my parents and yet they, too, are unique. Amazing.

Then I go lay down in my bed and reach out to hold the hand of a man who is very wise and yet loves me and is committed to me out of all the women in the world. I am blessed that I get to be with him for a lifetime. Amazing.

In the morning, I will begin another day and see more amazing things. I am learning not to take them for granted. God brings 'amazing' things in my life many of which won't be here again tomorrow so I must savor them today.

And suddenly there was a sound from heaven like a strong wind blowing, and it filled the whole house where they were saying and something like flames of fire appeared, divided and settled on each one of them, and they were all filled with the Holy spirit and began to speak in different kinds of languages just as the Spirit caused them to speak. And there were Jewish men of good reputation staying in Jerusalem. They were from every nation under heaven. And when this noise came about, the crowd came together and were confused, because each one was hearing them speaking in their own language. Acts 2:2-6 (HNT)

Though many witnessed this event that day and many heard Peter's words of repentance that came after this event, Scripture does not tell us that <u>all</u> acknowledged Jesus as Savior and not <u>all</u> gave God the credit for the amazing happenings of the day. Things haven't changed much in 2,000 years. I want to be open to 'see' the amazing events that come from God and acknowledge Him as the author and creator of amazing things…every day.

Question: What would go on my 'amazing list' today?

I can do all things through him who strengthens me.   Philippians 3:14 (ESV)

I've always thought that the gospel writer and physician, Luke, sat down with Mary and 'interviewed' her about the events of the birth of Jesus. His gospel is such a true and beautiful picture of this time.

This 15-year-old girl, named Mary, was a girl who had an obedient and humble heart – just what God was looking for in the mother of His Son. She was also a practical girl as she asks the angel how she is going to have a baby since she was a virgin.

And the angel answered her, "The Holy Spirit will come upon you, and the power of the Most High will overshadow you; therefore the child to be born will be called holy – the Son of God.   Luke 1:35 (ESV)

When God calls me to do a task for Him, do I put Him off because I don't see how it can be done? Why do I think God will have a problem supplying the money for a mission trip or tuition for school? Would the One who made the heavens and earth and everything between be stumped in finding a way for me to attend a Bible study EVERY Monday night? Or maybe God could locate Moses to lead His people to the Promised Land but surely He can't find a life mate for me without my going 'hunting' on my own!

So when they had come together, they asked him, "Lord, will you at this time restore the kingdom to Israel?" He said to them, "It is not for you to know times or seasons that the Father has fixed by his own authority. But you will receive power when the Holy Spirit has come upon you, and you will be my witnesses in Jerusalem and in all Judea and Samaria, and to the end of the earth." And when he had said these things, as they were looking on, he was lifted up, and a cloud took him out of their sight.   Acts 1:6-9 (ESV)

Jesus promised me the Holy Spirit and the power that would come with Him. The Holy Spirit reveals to me the very thoughts of God

But, as it is written, "What no eye has seen, nor ear heard, nor the heart of man imagined, what God has prepared for those who love him" – these things God has revealed to us through the Spirit. For the Spirit searches everything, even the depths of God. For who knows a person's thoughts except the spirit of that person, which is in him? So also no one comprehends the thoughts of God except the Spirit of God. Now we have received not the spirit of the world, but the Spirit who is from God, that we might understand the things freely given us by God. And we impart this in words not taught by human wisdom but taught by the Sprit, interpreting spiritual truths to those who are spiritual. The natural person does not accept the things of the Spirit of God, for they are folly to him, and he is not able to understand them because they are spiritually discerned.

1 Corinthians 2:9-14 (ESV)

God gave me Scripture. He gave me a mind to reason things out. He has given me history to teach me how things went with those before me. But He didn't stop there. He desired that He and I have a <u>personal</u> experience together. That HIS Holy Spirit touches my spirit and the experience would be eternal.

Question: Which is most important to you and why: Scripture, tradition, personal experience, or reason?

"Pray along these lines: 'Our Father in heaven, we honor your holy name. We ask that your kingdom will come now. May your will be done here on earth, just as it is in heaven. Give us our food again today, as usual ... "

Matthew 6:9-11 (TLB)

It is interesting, and yes, a bit troubling, that Jesus instructs me to pray – for bread enough for…today. Only. In this prayer, my past is only brought up to forgive my sins. My future is only about the temptations that may come my way and the assurance that God is not surprised by that either. My present, my today – God will provide enough 'bread', of everything that I need…for today.

And don't make me either rich or poor; just give me enough food for each day.

Proverbs 30:8 (NCV)

Jesus said the same thing that the 'Wisdom' of Proverbs said, *'enough food for each day'*! It is a trust issue. Trust God that He <u>knows</u> what I need for today and <u>knows</u> even what tomorrow will bring and has that in His hand also.

When things are going well, the 'bread' that God provides are like 'Twinkies' or 'Oreos' on my plate! The time is sweet. I want to just spend a lot of time with the Lord and enjoy the meal He has prepared for me. This is God's kitchen not His restaurant where I receive my 'daily bread'. It's not a restaurant because I don't come in expecting a menu that I order what <u>I</u> want but it is God's kitchen where <u>He</u> plans what <u>He</u> knows what I need. Some days have more vegetables where I receive lessons and some days have meat that I have to 'chew' and 'chew' and swallow in small bites so I don't choke! God's lessons of His love and mercy to me are sweet. His lessons of unconditional love and mercy that I extend to others in the same way that I want to receive it…are sometimes as palatable as cauliflower! The larger lessons of how He works and His way of wisdom require some 'chewing' on my part and take a little longer to 'digest'. And then there are those cups of suffering and pain that are sometimes so vile and difficult to look at. Jesus was given a cup like that. What did He do?

Jesus who knew the Father and trusted Him completely, looked at what the Father was giving Him that day for His 'bread' and said, "Oh, no! PLEASE give me something else!…But, I'll drink it ... with your help." (Matthew 26:39)

Yes, sometimes what is on my plate for this day is difficult to consume. The 'cup' may contain suffering and hardship that seems impossible to drink: the loss of a job, wrongful accusations of co-workers or even family and friends, the loss of someone you love and it hurts so much you may think you will never 'eat' again. Jesus has been there and He even asked the Father to take the cup from Him. Look at the Father's response:

An angel from heaven appeared to him and strengthened him. Luke 22:43

Whatever the Father serves me this day, I must take that step of trust in faith and <u>know</u> from my past experiences with Him that He will send me the strength I need…for today. I may never be exonerated in this world. I may never have all the answers to my questions in this world. But I will <u>always</u> have Jesus before me and His Holy Spirit surrounding me and my 'Abba Father' who loves me. I have what I need…for today.

Question: What has God 'served' to me today? Is it enough?

I wish that everyone were like me, but each person has his own gift from God. One has one gift, another has another gift.   *1 Corinthians 7:7 (NCV)*

The day after Christmas! When I was a child, this was the time to REALLY have fun! Christmas Day is when you had to wear good clothes and sit around at Grandma's and not get dirty and listen to the adults talk about the "old days" – which included telling embarrassing stories about your children! The day after Christmas meant I could go find all my friends and compare 'loot'. Yes, it was a time of trying not to admit that Debbie got something more 'groovy' than me – but I also remember being grateful that I didn't get those 'dorky shoes' that she got!!!

Paul in speaking to the Corinthian church is addressing the bottom line problem that the members were not affirming and encouraging each other in their different gifts. They were jostling for the 'greater seat' – seeking to be 'king of the hill'. Paul even admits that it would be easier for him if everyone was like him – in this case, single instead of married – but he acknowledges that all gifts from God are worthy and needed in the church.

This is why I remind you to keep using the gift God gave you when I laid my hands on you. Now let it grow, as a small flame grows into a fire. God did not give us a spirit that makes us afraid but a spirit of power and love and self-control.   *2 Timothy 1:6-7 (NCV)*

Here Paul tells me not to take my God-given gift and stick it in the back of my closet. God doesn't give us some disgusting 'fruitcake-like' gift. Jesus told us that the Father only gives good gifts to His children. I should use my God-given gifts to build God's kingdom in whatever way His Holy Spirit leads me.

Like the Magi who visited Jesus with their gifts, I am to lay the gifts He has given me down at His feet and say, "Speak, Lord, your servant is listening!"

Jesus was born in the town of Bethlehem in Judea during the time when Herod was king. When Jesus was born, some wise men from the east came to Jerusalem. They asked, "Where is the baby who was born to be the king of the Jews? We saw his star in the east and have come to worship him."

When King Herod heard this, he was troubled, as well as all the people in Jerusalem. Herod called a meeting of all the leading priests and teachers of the law and asked them where the Christ would be born. They answered, "In a town of Bethlehem in Judea. The prophet wrote about this in the Scriptures: 'But you, Bethlehem, in the land of Judah, are important among the tribes of Judah. A ruler will come from you who will be like a shepherd for my people Israel.'"...

After the wise men heard the king, they left. The star they had seen in the east went before them until it stopped above the place where the child was. When the wise men saw the star, they were filled with joy. They came to the house where the child was and saw him with his mother, Mary, and they bowed down and worshiped him. They opened their gifts and gave him treasures of gold, frankincense, and myrrh.   *Matthew 2:1-6, 9-11 (NCV)*

Questions: How did you share the Good News with someone this Christmas season?

Therefore, if anyone is in Christ, he is a new creation; the old has gone, the new has come! All this is from God, who reconciled us to himself through Christ and gave us the ministry of reconciliation: that God was reconciling the world to himself in Christ, not counting men's sins against them. And he has committed to us the message of reconciliation. We are therefore Christ's ambassadors, as though God were making his appeal through us. We implore you on Christ's behalf: Be reconciled to God. God made him who had no sin to be sin for us, so that in him we might become the righteousness of God. As God's fellow workers we urge you not to receive God's grace in vain. For he says,
"In the time of my favor I heard you, and in the day of salvation I helped you."
I tell you, now is the time of God's favor, now is the day of salvation.

2 Corinthians 5:17-6:2

As I come to the end of another year, I cannot help but review the events in my life. I have found that it's important to ask the Lord to shed His light of truth on this reflection but I think it's a good thing – a time of praise for all that the Lord has done. It is an opportunity to walk away from another layer of the 'old woman' in me and press on to the new creation that God is doing inside of me. God does a reconciliation inside of me, using the experiences in my past to refine the new woman that is in my future. Only God can do that so perfectly!

God's grace is always sufficient, sufficient for every experience – every circumstance. What is grace? It is that undeserved love that Jesus showed when He submitted to the Father's plan and walked that *Via Delarosa* – way of pain – to Calvary. Not only walked the way but also did it without anger or complaint. That same grace is right here for me. All day. Every day. Is my boss being unfair? Is my spouse being unreasonable? God's grace is sufficient. Did my church family forget to visit me when I had surgery? Was my name omitted from the list of choir members in the cantata? God's grace is sufficient. It's not a candy coating – it's a heart changing, real deal, eternal fix. It's God's grace.

Jesus told us that we are to love each other. And not just love those we like – but love our enemies, too!!! I need God's grace to do that! I surely cannot do it in my own strength!

Dear friends, let us love one another, for love comes from God. Everyone who loves has been born of God and knows God. Whoever does not love does not know God, because God is love. This is how God showed his love among us: He sent his one and only Son into the world that we might live through him. This is love: not that we loved God, but that he loved us and sent his Son as an atoning sacrifice for our sins. Dear friends, since God so loved us, we also ought to love one another. No one has ever seen God; but if we love one another, God lives in us and his love is made complete in us.   *1 John 4:7-12*

It's a complete circle. God loves me. He pours that love into me and it flows out of me onto and into others. They, in turn, see God's love in me and in turn love Him for what He has done. God's grace is sufficient for me AND everyone else I allow it to run through! GIVE GOD THE GLORY!!!

Suggestion: Make a list of your 'troubles' from this year. Fold it. Leave it behind with your worry. Leader: Burn them!

References

God continues to inspire His children to write and share His wisdom and knowledge with each other. These are <u>some</u> of the authors who are mentioned within the texts of the devotions. I pray that with your own Bible in hand, that you will utilize the wonderful resources that we have been given!

Bevere, John. <u>The Devil's Door</u>. Creation House. ISBN# 0884194426. 1997.

Chambers, Oswald. <u>My Utmost for His Highest</u>. Discovery House Publishers. Updated edition. ISBN# 0929239571. July 1992.

Dobson, James. <u>The New Dare to Discipline</u>. Tyndale House Publishers. ISBN# 0842305068. 1996.

Hill, Rev. Stephen. <u>Daily Awakenings</u>. Regal Books. ISBN# 0830725121. 2000.

Joyner, Rick. <u>Final Quest</u>. Whitaker House. ISBN# 0883684780. 1997.

Lucado, Max. <u>Come Thirsty</u>. Word Publishing Group. ISBN# 0849917611. 2004.

Lucado, Max. <u>In the Grip of Grace</u>. Word Publishing Group. ISBN# 0849911435. 1996.

Lucado, Max. <u>Traveling Light</u>. Word Publishing Group. ISBN# 0849912970. 2001.

Manning, Doug. <u>Don't Take My Grief Away</u>. Harper San Francisco. ISBN# 0060654171. 1984.

Omartian, Stormie. <u>Praying Through Life's Problems</u>. Integrity Publishers. ISBN# 1591450578. 2003.

Omartian, Stormie. <u>The Power of the Praying Wife</u>.
Harvest House Publishers, Inc. ISBN # 1565075722. 1997.

Omartian, Stormie. <u>The Power of the Praying Husband</u>.
Harvest House Publishers, Inc. ISBN # 0736905324. 2001.

Omartian, Stormie. <u>The Power of the Praying Parent</u>.
 Harvest House Publishers, Inc. ISBN# 1565073541. 1995.

Ravenhill, David. <u>The Jesus Letters</u>. Destiny Image.
ISBN# 076842173X. 2002.

Tatelbaum, Judy. <u>The Courage to Grieve</u>. Perennial.
ISBN# 0060911859. 1984.

Tenny, T.F. and Tenny, Tommy. <u>Secret Sources of Power</u>.
Destiny Image Publishers. ISBN# 0768450004. 2000.

Warnke, Mike. <u>Friendly Fire: A Recovery Guide for Believers
Battered by Religion</u>. Destiny Image. ISBN# 0768421241.
2002.

Westberg, Granger. <u>Good Grief</u>. Fortress Press.
ISBN# 0800611144. 1979.

Wilkinson, Bruce. <u>Prayer of Jabez</u>. Multnomah Publishers Inc.
ISBN# 1576737330. 2000.

Wilkinson, Bruce. <u>Secrets of the Vine</u>.
Multnomah Publishers Inc. ISBN# 1576739759. 2001.

www.ingramcontent.com/pod-product-compliance
Lightning Source LLC
Chambersburg PA
CBHW031612040426
42452CB00006B/489